Canva Guidebook

The Comprehensive Manual for Developing Your Brand, Marketing Materials, Presentations, Social Media Content, and Graphic Design Skills

Ben Calvin

CHAPTER ONE
AN OVERVIEW OF CANVA

Canva: What is it?

Anyone may create a wide variety of visual material using the online design platform Canva without needing to be highly skilled in graphic design. It is renowned for its user-friendly interface, which enables individuals, organizations, and groups to utilize it without any technological expertise. No matter how little or how much design expertise you have, Canva's tools and templates can help you quickly and effortlessly create designs that appear professional. The platform has grown to become one of the most well-known design tools worldwide since its release in 2013. It has a freemium business model, meaning that although many features are free, customers who subscribe to Canva Pro or Canva for Teams may access additional premium features, templates, and components.

Important Canva Features

Templates

Canva offers hundreds of pre-made templates for presentations, resumes, business cards, invitations, posters, social media posts, and more. These templates include well created designs, and users may alter the layouts, colors, fonts, and images to suit their requirements.

Drag-and-Drop Interface

One of Canva's biggest features is its drag-and-drop interface, which eliminates the need for complex tools or coding knowledge. Simply selecting items·such as text, photos, shapes, and icons and placing them on their creative canvas makes it straightforward and simple for people to create things.

Media Library

Canva offers a vast collection of design components, including audio and video clips, stock images, drawings, typefaces, shapes, and icons. Many of these sections are free; however access to the premium ones requires a contract.

Collaboration

Canva enables real-time cooperation so that many individuals may work on the same design simultaneously. For teams or projects that need input from several individuals, this is quite beneficial. Collaborative features include commenting, exchanging designs via links, and assigning roles such as editor or spectator.

Versatility

The tool may be used for both personal and professional objectives. Businesses may use Canva for branding, marketing, and promotional materials, while individuals can use it to create personal projects like image collages, greeting cards, and event invites.

Desktop and Mobile Compatibility

Canva offers mobile features and a web app for iOS and Android smartphones. Users may see and modify their ideas from any device, including a computer, tablet, or phone, thanks to cross-platform compatibility.

Canva Pro

Canva Pro offers customers additional capabilities including limitless storage, customized brand kits with unique fonts, colors, and logos, sophisticated creative tools, premium templates, and access to a wider media library.

The Reasons behind Canva Usage

Canva's popularity may be attributed to its ease of use and comprehension. Using professional design software, such as Adobe Photoshop and Illustrator, often requires a great deal of technical expertise and effort. Conversely, Canva is designed to be user-friendly for all users. For small companies, educators, students, marketers, and everyone else who wants to create visually appealing material without hiring a designer; this makes it an excellent option. For example, a small company owner might create advertising flyers or social media visuals using Canva instead of hiring a third party. It may be used, for instance, to create an eye-catching display for a class assignment.

Typical Applications

Social Media Content

Canva is widely used to create posts, stories, banners, and advertisements that are compatible with Facebook, Instagram, Twitter, LinkedIn, and TikTok. Designs are sized appropriately for each device thanks to its templates.

Marketing and Branding

Canva assists businesses in maintaining a consistent identity across all of their assets, including advertisements, brochures, business cards, and logos. The brand kit feature in Canva Pro is another tool that facilitates this process.

Educational Resources

Teachers and students often use Canva to create worksheets, infographics, presentations, and classroom posters.

Events and Personal Projects

Canva is often used to create customized graphics for birthdays, weddings, holidays, and other occasions, including greeting cards, image collages, and invites.

Video Editing

Although Canva's video editing features aren't as sophisticated as those found in specialist software, users can nevertheless create basic films with text overlays, music, and transitions.

The benefits of Canva

1. **Usability:** Even for beginners, the platform's design makes it simple to use.
2. **Affordability:** Compared to professional design software, the subscription plans aren't overly costly, and the free version offers a lot of capabilities.
3. **Variety of Options:** Canva can accommodate a broad variety of company demands thanks to its hundreds of templates and design features.
4. **Cloud-Based:** Users can update their creations from any location and share them with others fast thanks to Canva's cloud-based architecture.

5. **Customizability:** Although Canva offers pre-made templates, users are free to start from scratch and create original designs.

Restrictions

Canva is robust and adaptable, yet in certain aspects it falls short of professional design tools. For instance, it could not be as accurate and provide as many editing options as programs like Adobe Creative Suite. For complex projects, Canva's capabilities may not be sufficient for seasoned designers. However, Canva offers more than enough tools to meet the majority of daily creative requirements.

Comprehending the Interface of Canva

Even those who have never created anything before may easily create visuals that appear professional because to Canva's user-friendly interface. It is divided into many sections, each of which has a distinct function. Users may interact with the platform more easily as a result. Whether you're creating a multi-page presentation or a basic image for social media, the interface is designed to make it simple to locate all the tools you need.

The Home Page

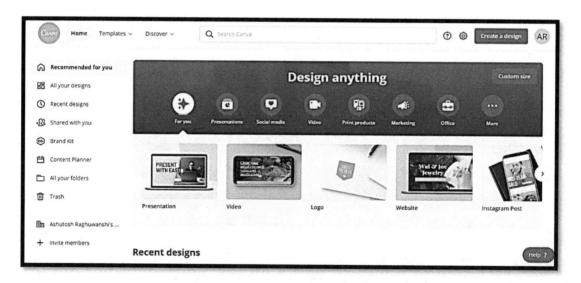

Whenever you first log in, you are sent to the main page. You may enter what you want to create in the search box at the top. If you need an Instagram post template, for instance, you just need to enter the keywords, and Canva will provide you with hundreds of options that meet your requirements. Tens of thousands of designs are arranged in templates so that you can easily discover what you need. Features display images, icons, print materials, applications, and other resources to assist you in creating what you want. You may learn more about design by taking advantage of Learn's blog pieces, short courses, and complete courses. Pricing explains how to create an account for a charity or become a pro. Below the search box are a variety of areas, including "Social Media," "Presentations," "Videos," "Posters," and more. These categories are designed to help you identify templates that are appropriate for your requirements fast. For example, if you choose "Presentations," you will see pre-made designs with customizable slide layouts in standard presentation size.

The Side Menu on Canva

If you need to reset after delving deeply into anything, you have an additional Home button. After that, you may organize and locate your designs under Your Projects. To keep things organized, create folders and let others to collaborate with you on the same files or designs. Tens of thousands of designs are available to you via templates, which may help you generate ideas. Based on your ideas, the recommended tab displays items that you may find appealing. Finding designs that you will collaborate on is simple using the Shared with you page. The Trash contains any designs, images, or videos that you have removed.

The Dashboard for Design

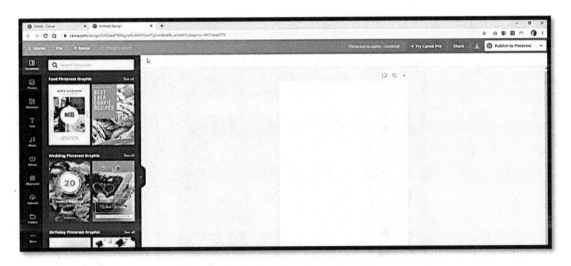

The design dashboard is the first thing you see when you begin a new project. Here's where the magic takes place. This is the primary space where you work on and modify your designs. The majority of the screen is occupied by the canvas, which displays the design itself. It's simple to drag and drop pieces, adjust their size, and move them about on this highly dynamic canvas. You can see the changes as they happen since all editing is done directly on the canvas, whether you're working on text, images, or shapes.

The Toolbar

The toolbar is visible above the canvas. It varies according on the task at hand. If you choose any text, for instance, the toolbar will provide options to alter the font, size, color, alignment, and even apply effects like outlines or shadows. The toolbar will include capabilities for cropping, resizing, flipping, and altering transparency. Without overcrowding the space, this dynamic toolbar ensures that you can always access all the tools you need.

The Sidebar

You may locate everything you need for your design with the aid of the sidebar, which is located on the left side of the screen. There are many tabs in this section, and each one has a distinct function. The first option, "Templates," allows you to browse among thousands of pre-made layouts according to the project type you are working on. You may utilize the vast array of forms, icons, photos, charts, frames, and grids found under the Elements tab, which comes next. You may upload your own images, movies, or audio snippets by selecting the Uploads option. In this manner, you may include distinctive or personal material into your designs. You may choose from a variety of pre-made font options and text styles under the Text tab. This makes it easy to include attention-grabbing headers and body content. In the Photos tab, you can also browse Canva's extensive collection of stock photos. The Backgrounds option offers a wide range of colors, patterns, and pictures for your design's backdrop. For projects with several pages, such as eBooks and slideshows, the bottom panel works well. Each page's thumbnail is shown here, allowing you to navigate between them and rearrange their order. You have complete control over the structure and flow of your project since it's simple to add or delete pages from this panel. One fantastic feature of Canva is that you can create anything using drag-and-drop without needing to know how to utilize complex tools or coding. For example, all you need to do to include an icon into your design is drag it into the page from the Elements tab. Once an icon appears, it's as simple as clicking and dragging to adjust its size, orientation, or position.

This approach gives seasoned designers enough flexibility while making Canva very user-friendly for novices. The ability to alter any component of the interface is also crucial. Whether you're working with text, graphics, or shapes, Canva offers tools that help you make the design really your own. For instance, you may alter text boxes' size, color, and style to fit your preferences. Along with altering the positioning and spacing, you may also apply effects like shadows or neon glows. You may trim photos, apply filters, and alter the color and contrast of pictures with Canva's built-in tools. Shapes and lines may be resized, colored, and rotated to suit your design. Additionally, Canva facilitates real-time collaboration, which is excellent for collaborative projects. By using the "Share" option located in the top right corner of the screen, you may allow others to see or modify your design. Using this tool, you may assign roles such as "Editor" or "Viewer" to ensure that everyone has the appropriate level of access. The ability to remark directly on the design allows project participants to easily exchange ideas and improve the project overall. When you're finished with your design, the UI makes it simple to share or export your work. Additionally, files in the PNG, JPG, PDF, MP4, and GIF formats may be sent via the "Share" button. Depending on your requirements, you may share the design on social media, download it to your computer or phone, or even print it using Canva's printing services.

Activities

1. What do you understand by Canva?
2. What are the Important Canva Features?
3. What are the typical applications of Canva?
4. What are the benefits of Canva?

CHAPTER TWO

HOW TO START RUNNING CANVA

Building an Account

To create and account, follow the steps below:

First Step: Get the app or go to the Canva website

To begin, visit the official Canva website at www.canva.com. You can also download the Canva app from the app store for your PC or smartphone. The app should function on the majority of devices since it is compatible with both iOS and Android.

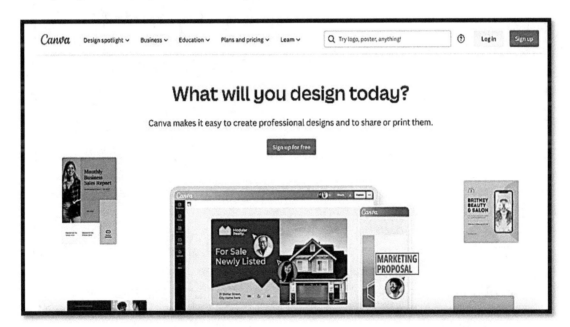

Second Step: Select the "Get Started" or "Sign Up" button.

The Canva webpage or app's launch screen has a large button that reads "Sign Up," "Get Started," or "Try Canva Free." You may begin establishing your account on the signup page after clicking this button.

Third Step: Select a Method of Sign-Up

Canva offers customers a variety of account creation options to meet their requirements. To join up, follow these steps:

- **Email Address:** People have always done it this way. You must provide a working email address and create a password. This is the greatest option if you want a Canva account that isn't linked to any other websites.
- **Google Account:** If you already have a Gmail account, creating a Canva account only requires a few clicks. You don't have to remember another password this way, which is useful.
- **Facebook Account:** You may use your Facebook details to register for Canva as well. Canva will link your account to your Facebook profile if you choose this option, making logging in simple.
- **Apple ID:** Another simple and secure method for Apple users to register is by using their Apple ID.

Which option you choose will depend on your preferences and how effectively you want to integrate with other platforms, since each has advantages of its own.

Fourth Step: Provide Your Information

You must complete a form if you want to join up using your email address. Typically, you'll provide this:

- **Full Name:** Enter your last and first names exactly as you would want them to appear on your Canva profile.
- **Email Address:** Please provide a working email address that you can access, since Canva may use it to send you updates, urgent alerts, or password reset instructions.
- **Password:** Choose a strong password that consists of both capital and lowercase letters, digits, and special characters to protect your data.

When you join up using Google, Facebook, or Apple, the majority of this information is pulled from your existing account. You save time by doing this.

Fifth Step: Accept the terms and conditions

Before you can proceed, Canva will require you to accept their terms of service and privacy statement. To obtain an idea of how Canva manages your information and what to anticipate from their website, you should briefly read these. When you're ready, click the "Confirm" button or check the box to proceed.

Sixth Step: If necessary, confirm your email address

Before allowing you to complete the enrollment process, Canva may require you to verify your email address. You will get an email with a link to complete this step if it is required. Click the link in the email after opening it. Your account is now fully enabled when you visit Canva as a result.

Seventh Step: Select the Type of Account

After creating an account, Canva will ask you to explain your preferred method of using the website. **These are typically the options:**

- **Personal Use:** This is excellent for those who want to create designs for social media postings, resumes, or greeting cards.
- **Business:** Designed for companies and employees in need of marketing materials, branding tools, and collaborative methods?
- **Education:** Designed for educators and learners, it includes resources for assignments and projects in the classroom.
- **Nonprofit:** This category is for organizations who want to create marketing collateral in order to generate funds or recognition.

Canva can personalize your experience by providing you with the appropriate templates, tools, and features by allowing you to choose an account type.

Eighth Step: Examine Canva's Paid and Free Plans

After creating your account, Canva can provide you the option to upgrade to Canva Pro, Canva for Teams, or Canva for Education. Although there are many helpful tools in the free edition, paying gives you access to premium templates, a vast media library, and other capabilities like content planning and brand kits. If you're unsure, you may begin with the free plan and upgrade if necessary.

After creating an account, logging in

After making an account, logging in is simple. When you return to the Canva website or use the app, you may input your Google, Facebook, Apple ID, and email address and password. Then, select "Log In." Many browsers and devices can store your login credentials for you if you want to save them so you can access them more quickly.

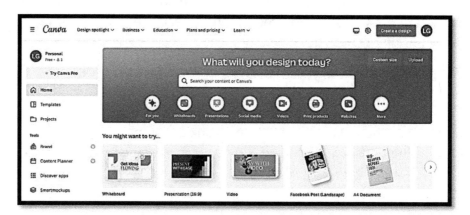

Employing Canva's Mobile Version

Now, let me briefly discuss the Canva app for smartphones. Additionally, you should install this app as the majority of people today use their phones for daily tasks and work rather than PCs. You may use the same credentials to access Canva's online and PC editions. After you do this, all of your logos, images, and design submissions will sync over. This implies that you may use the app on your phone to see whatever you create on your PC. The website lacks some of the functionality that the app has, and there are just a few minor differences. The only obvious difference between them is the size of the screen. We can see far more and prepare for larger projects at our workstations and laptops. Getting designs, organizing, and posting to social media while on the go is made simple by your phone's tiny screen. Both the Google Play Store and the Apple App Store provide the Canva app for smartphones. There will probably be an advertisement at the top of the page. Select Canva, then log in with your Canva credentials.

After that, your phone will open and display this screen:

The following are some ways that the PC and mobile versions of Canva differ:

- To draw, click the little purple circle in the lower right corner. The primary menu is located across the bottom, not to the left.

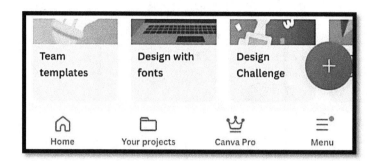

- When constructing, all of the template's components are at the bottom rather than the top.

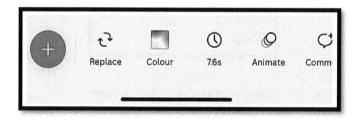

To access the components while creating, tap the little purple circle in the lower left corner of the screen. On the right side of the screen is a white circle that contains a number in a square, this enables you to see every page at once.

Creating a Canva Profile and Beginning Design

- Log into your Canva account.
- Select the "Profile" icon located in the top right corner of the screen.
- Select "Create Profile" from the menu.
- Enter your contact details, including your name and email address.
- Upload a cover photo and a profile image.

- Include a brief biography of yourself.
- Click "Save" to finish.

After creating your profile, you can begin creating content. Click "Create" and choose the kind of material you want to produce to do this. You can create a wide range of material using Canva, including brochures, presentations, and social media posts. Give your writing a title and a brief description if you plan to write anything. The description should make it apparent to readers what the content is about, and the title should be brief and concise.

Settings for Profiles

Modify your account name and Canva purpose

- From the main page, choose Settings. Verify that the Account tab is selected.
- Click "Edit" next to your name and type in a new one.
- Click Save to complete.
- To modify your Canva use, scroll down and find the purpose for which you want to use Canva.
- Select an option by clicking on the dropdown menu. The modifications will be instantly stored.

You should only use letters and not digits or special characters if you want your account name to appear in Canva emails (for instance, when you share or invite team members to a design).

Upload or Modify Your Profile Picture

- Click on your profile photo located in the top right corner of the homepage.
- Drag your mouse pointer over the current image. There will be a camera icon. Hit it.
- From your tablet or phone, choose the file you want to transmit, and then select "Open." Once the upload is complete, your profile image will be instantly updated.

Configuring the profile page for your Creator

As a Canva Creator, you have a public profile where others may see your templates and materials. **Modify the information on your page to advertise your company.**

- Click the gear icon in the top right corner of the homepage to access your Account Settings.
- From the side panel, choose "Public Profile".

- Modify your information. Use just lowercase letters and avoid spaces when entering the URL for your Canva profile.
- In order to complete, choose "Save changes."

You can see your profile by clicking on the link at the top of the page.

Unable to change your URL or display name?

Your URL name and your display name cannot be the same. Give them all unique names.

Change the Public Profile Picture

Click on your account icon on the site to modify your profile image. Then, to upload your photo, click on your account icon once again.

No Public Profile Page Is Available

Verify that you are in the Contributor or Creator brand.
- On the Canva homepage, click the account icon located in the top right corner.
- Move your cursor down until "Switch team." It displays all of the teams and brands you are associated with.
- Look for your Contributor brand name. Click to switch to it if there isn't ✓ next to it. After that, the page will reload.

Verify that you are in onto the correct account if you are unable to see your Contributor brand under Switch Teams.

Activities

1. Explain the steps to create and account
2. Explain the process of logging in after creating an account
3. Discuss the steps for Creating a Canva Profile and Beginning Design
4. Discuss the Settings for Profiles

CHAPTER THREE

THE ESSENTIALS OF DESIGN

Coming Up with a New Design

To begin working on a project, you will need to start a new canvas. You have two options.

- **Create your canvas from the beginning:** The "Create a Design" button in the top left corner is blue. Click on it. Select "Custom Size" and type in the desired width and height.
- **Select an already-made canvas:** You will need to create photos of a certain size if you are working on a project for a specific purpose, such as a Facebook advertisement. This is easy to accomplish. You may either scroll down the list or enter the name of the image to locate it. There are whiteboards for pins, email headers, restaurant menus, and pretty much anything else you would need. Click "Create a design."

Selecting the Appropriate Template

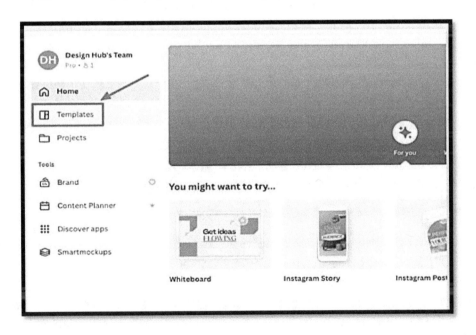

The pre-made layouts included in Canva's templates may be used as ideas for your own work. To maintain the design's balance, they include elements like images, text boxes, photographs, and placeholders that are thoughtfully positioned. Because templates eliminate the need to start from scratch, they are particularly helpful for those with limited time or limited creative skills. Choosing the appropriate template will guarantee that your material is both aesthetically pleasing and compatible with the platform. For instance, a party invitation may need vibrant colors and playful typefaces, whereas a corporate presentation requires a neat, serious design. Additionally, templates ensure that the appropriate formats and sizes are utilized for various platforms, such as written content, YouTube thumbnails, and Instagram posts.

How to Pick the Correct Template

Step One: Establish Your Goal

You should know what you want your design to accomplish before selecting a template. Consider these:
- **What am I producing?** Should it be a chart, flier, poster, résumé, or something else entirely?
- **Who am I trying to reach?** For whom are you doing this? Are they members of the general public, friends, students, or business clients?
- **What is the intended application of this design?** Will it be printed out and distributed, shown at a meeting, or shared online on social media?

How you respond to these questions will determine the kinds of templates you should investigate. Canva's templates are categorized by kind, making it simple to choose ones that suit your needs. **For instance:**
- There are social media templates for Facebook covers, Pinterest pins, and Instagram posts.
- Look at business card, presentation, and letterhead templates for usage in a professional setting.
- Canva provides choices for personal projects, such as party posters, wedding invites, and picture collages.

Step Two: Make Use of the Search Bar

You may utilize Canva's search bar to locate templates that meet your demands once you know what you want to achieve. Type "event flyer" or "party invitation," for instance, if you require a design for an event, and Canva will provide a choice of designs that fit your query. You won't have to navigate through irrelevant alternatives in this manner. **In the search area, you may also type phrases associated with themes, styles, or colors. For instance:**
- Seek for a "minimalist presentation" if you're looking for something straightforward and innovative.

+ Use phrases like "summer party flyer" or "Christmas card" for projects with a seasonal or holiday theme.

Step Three: Select the Appropriate Measurements

You don't need to alter your design to suit Canva templates since they are already the appropriate size for certain platforms or file formats. Because the incorrect size might detract from the appearance of your material, this step is particularly crucial for digital projects. **For instance:**
+ **Social Media:** Pinterest pins must be 1000x1500 pixels vertical, and Instagram posts must be 1080x1080 pixels square.
+ **Print Projects:** Standard card sizes are utilized for business cards, while A4 or letter-size paper is often used for posters and flyers.

If you have special requirements, you may choose templates by size or use the "Custom Size" option to create a blank canvas with the precise measurements you want.

Step Four: Take Your Personal Style into Account

Your audience and message should complement the template's design. Canva offers a wide range of designs, from bold and colorful to clean and basic.

To choose the appropriate one:
+ **Seek Color Themes:** For instance, a lively and entertaining template may be appropriate for a children's party invitation, while a somber report would benefit from a more muted color palette.
+ **Evaluate Font Selections:** While designs for event posters utilize large, ornate fonts, formal presentations and resumes look better with more conventional fonts.
+ **Layout:** Templates with plenty of moving images are ideal for artistic projects, while plain layouts with lots of empty space are great for corporate projects.

Step Five: Examine a Variety of Choices

Examine many templates before selecting one. A template will open in Canva's designer when you click on it. **You may then examine its components and structure in further detail. Consider this:**
+ Does this template provide the appropriate quantity of text and images for my needs?
+ Is it simple to alter the placeholder elements?
+ Does the general aesthetic match my vision?

To choose the finest template for your project, see the designs of many templates before purchasing them.

Step Six: Give Customization Priority

Although templates are designed to save time, they should nevertheless seem unique to your project. Seek for templates that provide several customization options. With Canva, you can alter almost every aspect of a template, including the layouts, colors, fonts, and photos. To make certain templates work for you, however, you may need to make more adjustments than others.

For instance:
- Changing a design with areas for five photographs might be challenging if you only have two to add.
- Changing templates with complex graphics may take longer if you need to adhere to a certain color scheme or style.

Select a template that will provide a solid foundation for your design while allowing for easy modification.

Common Errors to Steer Clear of

- **Selecting a Template Only on the Basis of Looks:** While the template's appearance is vital, its functionality is much more crucial. Spending time and energy on a gorgeous design that doesn't fit your objectives or content might be a waste.
- **Disregarding the intended audience:** Your message may suffer if the design style deviates from what the audience is used to. Creating a business report with a humorous template, for instance, would not seem professional.
- **Ignoring the Template's Dimensions:** Pixels, cropping issues, or poor print quality might result from using the incorrect size for your instrument or media. Before proceeding, be sure you double-check the dimensions.
- **Ignoring Customization:** You risk creating a dull, uninspired look if you employ a template without making any modifications. A few little adjustments that may have a significant impact include altering the typefaces or adding your company colors.

Choosing a Social Media Template: A Real-World Example

Imagine posting on Instagram to inform folks about a summer deal. Start by typing "summer sale Instagram post" into Canva's search box. The site will display many layouts, most of which use large typefaces, vibrant hues, and seasonal imagery such as views of the beach or sun. Examine a few options and choose the one that best suits your brand's tone. Select a design that is simpler and uses fewer colors if your company is straightforward. Select a design with vibrant gradients or dynamic icons if you want to have more fun. You may customize a template by adding your own picture, altering the colors to fit your brand, and adding text that is relevant to your offer.

Preserving Your Design and Additional Choices

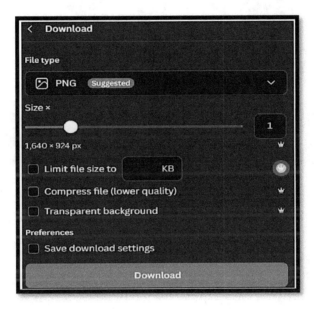

Your design just has to be saved once you're finished. The finish of your adventure is nearly here. To save your design, click the "Save" icon in the top left corner of the page. Select the file type, click "Download," and then click "Download" at the bottom to transmit it. After a short wait, you'll be finished! **There are many options to distribute your design on Canva, including but not limited to the following:**

 ⊹ Saving the design to Dropbox or Google Drive.
 ⊹ Directly posting the design to various social media networks.
 ⊹ Providing others with a sharing link so they may work together.
 ⊹ Purchasing prints directly from Canva, which will be delivered to your home?

Examining the Editing or Design Tools

Canva's design tools are organized into many divisions to aid in various stages of the creative process. To bring your creative ideas to life, you may use these tools to alter text, pictures, colors, layouts, and other elements. The tools may be used for any kind of design project, including invitations, business shows, and social media posts.

Before you begin editing, let us assist you in becoming acquainted with the design or editing tools. This will guarantee that your task runs without a hitch. After you choose a template or design, Canva will direct you to the Design Page. **The following items are located in the Toolbar on the left side of this page:**

A. Design: Styles offers you font sets, color palettes, or combinations of typefaces and color palettes to use in your design, or you may utilize design templates that you can modify to match your canvas.

B. The elements: Thousands of distinct design aspects are easily accessible with this application. Stickers, pictures, films, music, charts, surveys, frames, mockups, artificial intelligence (AI) image generators, and shapes are a few examples of these design components. Additionally, the search box makes it simple to locate any design-related information you want. You just need to choose a design feature to make changes to it. After that, a little toolbar will appear on top of the page. This element may be altered by changing its color, adding a border, reshaping it, cropping it, rotating it, altering its transparency, rearranging it, and even selecting an animation.

C. Text: Without a doubt, some writing is necessary for any design. To add text, just press the "Text" bar. You may include body content, a subheading, or a title. Just like you may alter the design elements, you can alter the text as well. Simply touch on the text to make changes, and a little horizontal menu will appear at the top of the page. In addition to changing the text's size, alignment, usage of text effects, location, and animation, you can also alter the text's color, font, style, and case.

D. Uploads: You may use this function to add images, movies, audio files, or gifs from your computer to your design. You might also add objects using Google Photos, Dropbox, or Google Drive.

E. Draw: You have greater flexibility to create your design whatever you want thanks to this feature. Using digital sketching tools including a pen, pencil, marker, and eraser, Draw enables you to give your design life. Additionally, you may alter the drawing tools' color, size, and transparency. Other editing tools may appear when you touch on a word or element. Tapping on an element or text will cause a smaller menu to display on top of it. You have the option to use additional widely used editing tools, such as copy, paste, duplicate, delete, comment, link, or lock.

Comprehending Additional Tools

- Tools for image editing so you can work with pictures and graphics.
- Tools for choosing and implementing color schemes.
- Tools for layout and alignment to help you arrange your design components.
- Filters and effects to improve images.
- Tools for animation for interactive, dynamic designs.
- Collaboration tools for group projects.

You can access these tools from the toolbar, side panels, or context menus, and they all work flawlessly with Canva's design center.

Tools for Editing Images

Images are frequently the most crucial component of a design, and Canva's image editing tools allow you to alter drawings and photos to suit your aesthetic. **Among the salient characteristics are:**

- **Upload and Insert Images:** You can upload images from your computer or use their extensive collection of stock photos and drawings.
- **Resizing and Cropping:** Images can be resized and cropped to fit into frames and grids or to highlight specific areas.
- **Filters and Adjustments:** Canva offers pre-made filters to alter the mood or tone of your images. You can also change color, contrast, saturation, and other things by hand.
- **Backdrop Remover:** This premium program allows you to remove the backdrop of a picture with a single click. Cutouts and translucent overlays are excellent uses for it.
- **Grids and Frames:** You may create unique shapes or well-organized layouts by dragging and dropping images into frames or grids.

About Color Tools

The tone and meaning of your design are greatly influenced by the colors you choose.
It is easy to utilize and switch up color schemes using Canva's color tools:
- **Color Picker:** Text, backgrounds, and forms may all be given solid colors by using the color selections. You have the option of selecting pre-existing colors or entering hexadecimal digits for accuracy.
- **Brand Colors:** Users of Canva Pro may create a brand kit that saves their company's colors for easy usage in all creations.
- **Gradients:** Use gradient overlays to give portions or backdrops a contemporary, vibrant appearance.
- **Transparency:** Modify the opacity of an element to layer or add subtle effects.

Tools for Layout and Alignment

For designs to seem balanced and professional, they need to be put out and aligned appropriately.
Canva includes features that can help you organize and line up elements:
- **Snapping and Grid Lines:** Canva provides alignment cues to assist you in positioning items as you move them around.
- **Group and Ungroup:** Place numerous things in a group to move or resize them as a single unit.
- **Arrange and Layering:** Put items in a new order to move them ahead or backward.
- **Resize Tool:** Are you a Canva Pro user? If so, the resize tool enables you adjust the scale of your design to match multiple formats, like changing an Instagram post into a Facebook banner.

Effects and Filters

There are effects and filters in Canva that may make your designs more creative and professional:
- **Image Effects:** To give photographs a distinctive appearance, employ effects like duotone, vignette, or pixelate.
- Text effects, such as neon, glitch, or shadow, may be used to highlight a word.
- **Advanced Filters:** Canva enables you adjust key components of a photo, like its color or temperature, to have greater control over how it appears.

Animation Tools

Canva's animation features enable you bring your drawings to life for projects that need to move:

- **Element Animation:** You may provide certain components, including text or pictures, animations like fade, slide, or bounce.
- **Page Transitions:** To create a seamless visual narrative, you may include page transitions into designs that have several pages.
- **Export Options:** Animated creations may be saved as GIFs or films, which you can subsequently share in presentations or on Instagram.

Features of Collaboration

Canva offers team project features that facilitate collaboration:

- Real-time editing allows many people to work on the same design simultaneously, and changes are immediately visible.
- **Commenting:** Team members may immediately remark on the design to provide recommendations or criticism.
- In order to restrict who may view what, assign responsibilities such as "Editor" or "Viewer."

Configuring Folders for Your Designs

You may create groups in Canva to arrange your designs according to various aspects of your personal or professional life. The "Your Projects" option makes it simple to see your most recent designs and locate the items you've shared. This is located next to the Home tab on the left side of the screen. **The components on this page are arranged as follows:**

- Recent
- Folders
- Designs
- Images
- Videos

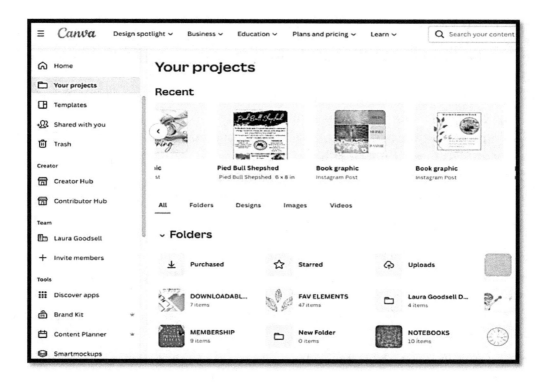

Everything you've created or shared is at the bottom of the page. It's the ideal location to access everything and serves as the center of your account.

Making Folders

There are already three folders in your account. They are as follows:
- **Purchased:** Everything you've purchased that wasn't included by your Pro membership is kept in this area.
- **Starred:** This contains any components or images you like and want to use at a later time.
- **Uploads:** All of the pictures and videos you upload to your account are stored there.

Both the Pro and Free editions come with an infinite number of folders, not only the three listed. **You may give them whatever name you choose. To create a new folder, do the following actions:**
- **Click the cross in the upper right corner. This will display a menu that says "Add new":**

- Press the icon for the folder.
- Give your folder a name.

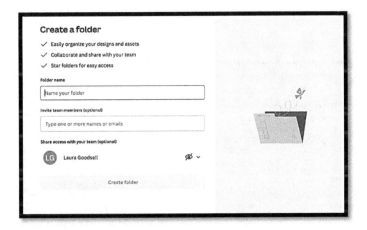

If you're not planning to form a team, don't bother about the second option. Only a basic folder will be created for this practice.

- Press the "Create Folder" button located at the very bottom.
- The Folders section of the website will now include your folder. You may alter a folder's appearance by clicking on it or the three dots that appear next to it.

To make your new folder the primary folder, you can also click the star symbol next to its name. It will become yellow. It will now show up on the left menu bar. It works well for everyone, and you may create as many files as you want. To conserve even more space, you may create folders up to five layers deep inside of files. Finally, the Folders option allows you to share a folder with a team member. However, because you can't share a folder with someone who isn't on your team, they must already have a Canva account. We've previously covered Canva's definition, how to utilize it, how to create an account on a computer and a phone, and the differences between the two primary Canva accounts. Now that we are working on our ideas in groups, they are more structured. Let's examine the Content Planner next.

Using the Content Planner to Arrange Content

For those that utilize social media and organize their postings, this Canva tool is fantastic. Posts created in Canva may be scheduled to appear on various social media platforms at various times. This implies that adding your material doesn't need you to register for other websites and applications. It is located on the main page's right side. However, if you are on Free, you will not be able to utilize this option. You may receive a 30-day free trial to determine whether you enjoy it enough to utilize it again. You may choose between months at the top of the Content Planner, which is organized like a calendar. At a glance, you can see where and when you intend to publish. Major holidays and global events are also displayed. Simply click on the event name to get a list of templates that have previously been created for that date if you need to create anything for it:

I was sent to the International Yoga Day website by this link. I may then start writing my article on International Yoga Day by clicking on the following:

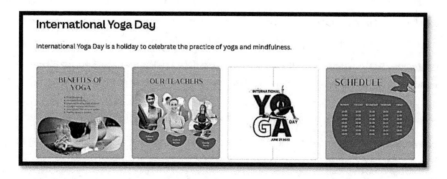

Making and Planning a Post

I'll walk you through the process of scheduling material for your social media connections since there are many methods to do this with Canva. To create a post, all you have to do is create an image and choose a date on the calendar. My designs appeared at the top when I clicked on the date I intended to utilize. A list of pre-made templates was located at the bottom. Another option is to start afresh in the center to the right. I'll use an already-made template this time:

It will open in the standard view for changing templates as soon as I choose one. Now, I can alter the text, images, and colors to better suit my brand.

You may choose a time after you have finished editing your template.

In the upper right corner, click the Share button:

A drop-down menu will be present. To locate the Schedule button, you may need to choose "More" at the bottom.

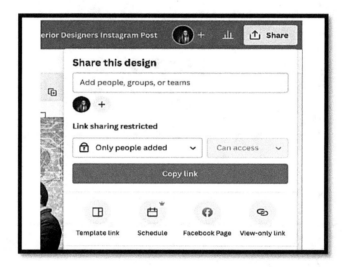

All of your options, including the Schedule tab and all of the social media platforms you may publish directly to, will be visible after you select the "More" button. All of your options in Canva are located here. When you see "Schedule," click on it after scrolling down. The Social section will be where it will be. You may then choose your channel, create your message, and modify the time and date you want it to go live using the boxes that appear. Clicking on the date will bring up a calendar. You may choose the time once you've decided on a date. After that, you may choose which channel to see. You must now link Canva to your social media accounts. The only difficult one is the one involving Facebook. You must log into Facebook and allow Canva to log in on your behalf. Additionally, you may link to publish directly to Instagram, the most widely used website. Joining a Creator account is the one thing you cannot do, however. However, they often simply want your Canva login credentials. If you are already signed in on another computer, it may connect itself. You may accomplish this by clicking the "Select a channel" option at the bottom of the list. After you sign up, it will appear at the top, and you may choose the channel you want to use:

Ultimately, your message should be written as you would on a social networking platform. With Canva, you can even limit how many characters you have. You can see how many words you used on each page at the very bottom right. Facebook allows you to use 5,000 characters, but Twitter allows you to use 280. At this point, you have the option to click Schedule or save your post as a draft for later editing. These choices are directly visible on the Content Planner calendar. To transmit the same post to another website after creating the design, click the "Make a copy" option. This button may only be used once each station.

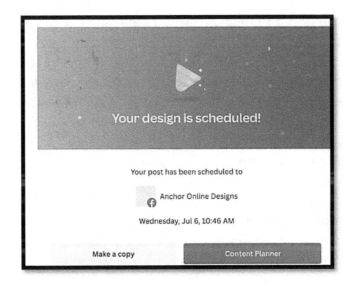

In the Content Planner, we will examine our post. All of the blogs I had planned are now visible. If you move your cursor over one, it will indicate the time and location of its destination. It is possible to schedule several posts for various locations on the same day. **Each platform will have a tiny symbol shown so you can see where everything is ready to upload:**

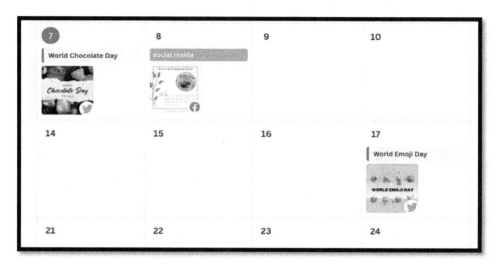

Any post you have prepared may be changed if necessary. The scheduled post will show up in Content Planner when you click on it, and you may edit it. When you're finished, just click Save and Schedule.

Other Methods for Scheduling and Posting

I thought it would be useful to briefly review the different methods that Canva can be used to prepare and publish to social media platforms that follow much the same steps. **Canva may be used on desktops and phones for the following two purposes:**

- Creating a plan is the initial step, but don't choose a date in the Content Planner just yet. Launch a fresh template and create your illustration. Next, go to the menu and choose "Schedule."
- Secondly, you may publish on any website immediately; there is no need to organize anything. To share, just click "Share" and choose your platform from the list. The "Arrange" button will be replaced with a "Publish now" button on the subsequent screen. You are not required to save your photos to your computer or phone before sharing them on social media. You may still use this drop-down to prepare for the following if you click on the little calendar icon in the lower left corner:

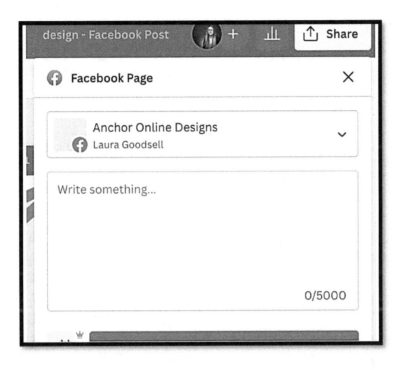

Planning and writing many pieces at once may save you a great deal of time. You may use this to help you choose what to write every day. One excellent tool that might assist you with your company is the Content Planner. Because it's a component of Pro, it's also free.

Activities

1. Discuss how to Pick the Correct Template
2. What are Common Errors to Steer Clear Of?
3. What is the Real-World Example Choosing a Social Media Template?
4. What are Other Methods for Scheduling and Posting?

CHAPTER FOUR
ABOUT CANVA MOBILE APP

The Canva App's Essential Features

The Home, Projects, Templates, and Canva Pro panels comprise the major section of the program. Let's review each section and its contents.

The Home Screen

The first item you see when you log in and launch the app is called "Home," so let's start there. It's quite easy to use since it appears like other social applications. The menu button is located at the top of the screen. It allows you to do some of the same tasks as the tabs, such as using templates and projects. You can only access Brand Hub and Content Planner as a Pro member. But you can also link more sophisticated programs and applications, like Smartmokups, to Canva. Beside the options is a search bar. You may use keywords to locate templates or projects that you have already completed. You may see the thousands of templates that are included with the program by clicking on the tabs below that. Depending on how you use Canva, "For You" will change every time you use the app, just as Spotify does. It will often display your most recent work along with various design sizes and templates that you may find useful. Each one will have a conspicuous label indicating its purpose. In other tabs, you may begin working on other templates, such as those for presentations, social media, movies, prints, and more. If you click on any of them, the website will alter to show you all the things you can do about that topic.

There are many methods to begin creating a fresh image from the home screen. Clicking on a template you like will open a new window where you can start editing it. Click on the desired design type, such Post or Video on Instagram, to begin creating a design. This page gives you the option to start from scratch or choose a template. Additionally, to restart, click the purple plus (+) symbol at the bottom of the screen. When you press it, you may choose the size (Custom or something like Facebook Post). A fresh, vacant spot will then show up.

The Screen for Projects

On the Projects page, you can see everything you've created on your computer, phone, or account. Your cloud-stored data, images, and ideas are visible to you. Each sketching image has two buttons in the top right corner. The three dots symbol opens a menu with several choices, including Edit; Make a Copy, and Share, while the arrow icon allows you to download the image.

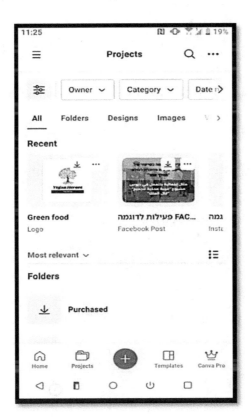

Keep in mind that Edit will alter your previous image. If you enjoy your design and would want to save it for later use, click "Make a Copy" instead.

The Screen of Templates

This one is more about templates; however it's similar to the main screen. Using the buttons at the top, you may browse each template or by topic. You may also see the themes that other Canva users have chosen, such Juneteenth or Earth Day. Seasons or holidays are often to blame. Features Collections, Trending Near You, New on Canva, and more sections are available. They're all designed to inspire you.

The screen of Canva Pro

If you pay for the service, you may see the final image. Options like Brand Kit, Premium Content, and social media programs are available here.

Make Your Own Design and Adjust It

Let's now discuss the tools available for creating pictures. Select a template to get started. We made advantage of an Instagram post. Note that not every template is compatible with a free account. Look for templates without the terms "Pro" or "Paid." You may alter any aspect of this image by clicking on the text, images, background, or shapes. Additionally, you may move it about, and the software will assist you with aligning objects in the center of the photo or with other objects. The controls for Undo and Redo are located in the top left corner. They resemble a pair of circular lines pointing in opposite directions. Click on any of the modifications you made that you dislike. A new set of options appears when you touch on a different area of the screen. The bar at the bottom of the screen contains them. This image has a "Replace" button on it. Pressing it allows you to choose a photo from Canva, snap a picture with your camera, or upload one from your phone's gallery.

Additionally, you may trim the image, apply effects and colors, make it move, and more. Press Edit after you've tapped a text area once to make changes. You may then alter the layout, size, style, and other elements. The Nudge tool has a significant impact. You can only move objects by one pixel at a time using the direction buttons. Compared to a touch screen, this is more precise. Additionally, you can use the addition (+) button to add new elements to the design. From that page, you may access all of your files, add music and images, change the background, and modify the template (which will replace the existing template).

Share or Download Your Canva Design

Now is the moment to utilize the image (or film) that you have meticulously altered to perfection. Press the buttons at the top of the screen to do that. The up button allows you to share the image with others, while the down arrow stores it to your phone. One of the best features of the Canva app is the Share button. You may email your finished photo directly to friends or coworkers via Slack or WhatsApp. You may also upload your photo directly to Instagram or TikTok by clicking the "Share" button. You would need to transfer the image to your phone first if you were on a computer. If you have a Pro account, you can even schedule the post to appear on social media at a certain time.

Utilizing Frames and Grids

Canva Grids

Using Canva's grids makes creation enjoyable and simple. Grids make it easier to organize text, images, videos, and colors into tidy groupings. They give any design a polished, completed appearance. Whether you are creating a marketing flyer, a mood board, or a picture collage, grids provide a simple framework to help ideas stand out. For those that want to get started, Canva offers a variety of grid options that are accessible straight from their site. Single-frame grids are ideal for basic designs, whereas multi-frame grids allow users to combine various elements. As a result, even novice designers may create designs that look fantastic. Grids may be utilized to convey tales; they are not simply boxes. To highlight certain regions of a photo, designers might use grids to frame those areas, add color, or even organize pieces. You may quickly transform a basic design into a visually appealing one by investigating the many applications for grids.

Getting to Canva's Grid Tools

Canva's grids facilitate the creation of tidy, expert graphics. They provide a straightforward method of organizing many pictures or features. Grids are simple for users to use on both computers and mobile devices. Open a new or existing design in Canva to get started. Examine the Canva editor's left side. You'll see options like Elements, Text, and Photos. Select the components. Once inside, type "grids" into the search field. A list of single-frame and multi-frame grids is shown below. Individuals may choose the kind that best suits their design. Another option is to just enter "grids" into the primary search field. You don't have to navigate through the sections to discover grid tools thanks to this functionality. A grid immediately adds to its design as a user clicks on it. They may then adjust the grid's dimensions and placement to suit their artwork.

Simply drag images or videos onto the grid. By itself, this operation cuts and fits them exactly. The Canva Help Center offers more guidance on how to use grids if you run across any issues. YouTube offers video tutorials that demonstrate how to do a task, which may aid in learning.

Choosing the Proper Grid for Your Project

If you choose the correct grid in Canva, it may greatly aid your creative job. Grid patterns vary, and pre-set and bespoke grids are available options. Selecting the appropriate one will improve the appearance of your project.

Grid Types and Configurations

There are several sizes and forms of grids. Common design components include collage grids, single-image grids, and multiple-photo layouts. Every kind has a distinct purpose. Grids with only one image are excellent for highlighting a single image. The greatest approach to showcase a collection of images or convey a narrative is using multi-photo arrangements. Additionally, grids come in a variety of forms and sizes. There are square, oblong, and even circular grids. Circular grids offer social media postings a distinctive appearance. Selecting the appropriate shape will be aided by the overall appearance and the material you want to highlight.

Comparing Custom and Pre-Set Grids

Canva artists have the option of using pre-made grids or creating their own. You are allowed to modify custom grids to suit your requirements. The grid's empty spaces and sizes may be altered by users to fit their requirements. For those that have a clear idea of how they want your plan to appear, this is ideal. Pre-set grids simplify the design process by providing you with pre-made options. They're excellent for novices or those with limited time. Without requiring numerous adjustments, pre-made grids assist ensure that the makeup is harmonized. When choosing between the two, consider the skill level and the requirements of the project. Whether you use an existing layout or a custom grid, Canva provides the tools you need to create amazing graphics.

Including Grids in Your Painting

You may organize components in your Canva design more aesthetically pleasingly by using grids. Text, photos, and other components may be easily arranged using grids, which expedites the design process and raises interest in completed projects.

Drag and Drop Grid Components

Grids may be used immediately by dragging and dropping them onto your artwork. Enter "grids" into the search field to find grids on Canva. After selecting your preferred grid, click and drag it onto your artwork. This operation creates the grid, which may include images, videos, or color blocks.

Modifying Grid Dimensions

Once the grids are on the artwork, it's simple to adjust their size. You may adjust the grid's size by dragging the handles that show up on the sides when you click on it. The designer may ensure that the grid matches the rest of the project by scaling it to fit precisely within the desired arrangement.

Content Alignment and Resizing

Grid sizes in Canva may be altered to suit the requirements of your project. Users may easily adjust the grid's size by using the "Resize" handle. With the use of this function, the designer may adjust the grid's size to suit their preferred layout, ensuring that the text and pictures inside each grid area are both readable and the proper size.

Adding Pictures to Grids

You can organize images in a variety of ways using Canva's grids. By clicking on the desired location inside the grid, users may add images to the grid. To see the available photos, they may choose Photos from the side panel. Instead, they may click Uploads and upload their own. A picture will be quickly scaled to fit if you drag and drop it into a grid space. Another advantage is that you may drag a new image over an existing one to rapidly swap between them. You don't have to start from scratch because of this.

Text Overlay on Grids

Adding text on top of grids is a simple way to add flair or information to projects. After selecting a grid, users may choose several text styles by clicking Text on the side panel. They may alter the color, size, and style by typing directly on the grid. Adjust the text box to match the design since positioning is crucial. To make it simpler to read, this might entail moving it to a less crowded area of the image. Shadows and borders help make text stand out more against a variety of backdrops.

Stacking Different Grids

Stacking grids on top of one another allows you to create designs with a variety of components. Designers may easily organize material into rows and columns by piling grids on top of one another, allowing each segment to showcase distinct elements. This technique allows you additional creative options by superimposing graphics, text, and pictures on top of one another. To start stacking grids, choose the foundation grid. Select a grid with the appropriate amount of frames to overlay the first grid. To make it fit in the basic grid, adjust the size and placement. This approach ensures a neat and orderly structure, which is ideal for presentations or pictures that include several subjects.

Canva frames

Canva's frames feature is crucial for creating vibrant, dynamic graphics. They provide users with placeholders that enable them to creatively arrange images inside a shaped space, improving the appearance of any project.

The Fundamental Ideas of Frames

Frames on Canva are essentially empty containers that may accommodate images or photographs. People may easily arrange their images in different forms and patterns using these frames. A image will alter its form to match the frame when it is dragged over it. This feature allows you to make adjustments quickly without using complex editing tools. It is a helpful option for any design task since users may quickly change the images within the frames. It makes design simple and enjoyable for users of all skill levels.

Various Frame Types Are Available

Each of the several frames available on Canva works well for a certain kind of design. Users should choose the Elements tab and scroll down until they reach the frames section. They may choose among letters, rectangles, circles, and even non-real forms.

Enhancing Your Design Using Frames

Canva frames allow users to clip images into shapes that improve the appearance of creations. This section teaches users how to locate frames, position them, and adjust their sizes in their design projects.

Searching for Frames using the Search Bar

Users must first open their design project in order to locate frames in Canva. On the side tray of the editor, they need to choose the "Elements" tab. using the search field, users may key in "frame." A selection of frames will appear for them to choose from. There are several options to suit the requirements of any design since the frames are available in a wide variety of forms and designs.

How to Attach Frames to the Canvas

You may add a frame directly on the canvas by clicking on it after selecting one. The frame may be moved by dragging and dropping it to the desired location. The placement of the frame should be carefully considered to ensure that it complements other design components. Pictures will be stored in the frame. Users may click and drag images from Canva's collection or their own uploads into the frame. This gives the image a polished appearance and ensures that it fits precisely within the frame form you choose.

Repositioning and Resizing Frames

Changing the size of a frame is simple once it is in place. The corner buttons may be used to adjust the frame's size when someone clicks on it. The dimensions of the frame are maintained by holding down the Shift key while making adjustments. One technique to move the frame is to click and drag it to a new location on the picture. Canva has snap-to-grid tools and grid lines for precise placement.

Personalizing Frames

Users may create designs that are really original and their own by altering the frames in Canva. By altering colors, adding effects, and placing frames over other parts, you can make your creations stand out and showcase your own style.

Altering the Colors of the Frame

Altering the color of frames may significantly alter their appearance and help them blend in with your design's concept. While some frames allow users to choose the colors, others have predetermined hues. To modify a frame's color, click on it and locate the "color palette" button. If the frame allows you to alter the colors, you can see this function. Next, decide which colors complement your overall design idea.

Enhancing Frames Using Effects

Effects provide frames additional intricacies and improve their appearance, which adds interest to any design. Shadows, glows, and outlines are some effects that provide depth. To add effects, click on the frame and go to the effects panel. Here, users may experiment with various settings, such the shadow's intensity or the glow's brightness. The design shouldn't be diminished by these effects, but they also shouldn't be overpowering.

Combining Frames with Additional Components

Layering is the process of adding frames to other design components, such as text, shapes, or images. This technique creates a visually appealing and rich layout. Select the frame first, and then drag it over the areas of your painting that you like to highlight. To decide whether section should go on top or below, it's crucial to utilize the arrange tool. This will assist in setting the proper visual ordering.

Using Pictures and Frames

Adding and altering images to improve any design is simple using Canva's frames. Users may easily upload photographs, modify their fit, and replace them. Use these steps to start working with images and frames.

Adding Pictures to Frames

Users should first choose the desired frame from the Canva components collection. They may search for images in the Canva editor's Photos section or upload their own images using the Uploads page. A picture will instantly snap into position if you select it and then drag it over the desired frame. In addition to saving time, this simple technique ensures that the image fits the frame without requiring any adjustments.

Changing Pictures inside Frames

Users may alter a photo to make it seem exactly like their design after placing it in a frame. To highlight certain aspects, they may drag the image around in Canva and zoom in or out. By clicking on the frame, they may access these options by bringing up a toolbar. They may eliminate undesired portions of the image or zoom in on key areas using the zoom tool. To move the image about in the frame, users may also wish to click and drag it. They may create a well-balanced and attractive layout by doing this.

Changing Pictures in Frames

The process of changing a photograph is simple and fast. To replace the image in a frame, just drag a new photo over an old one. This operation will automatically replace the photo without requiring the user to remove it first.

Making Personalized Frame Layouts

Using frames makes it simple to alter the appearance of plans. To fit their design requirements, users may alter the frames' size, placement, and appearance. There are many distinct frame types available on Canva, ranging from basic borders to more unusual forms. It is simple to alter the frames' color and size to match the project's aesthetic. You may organize text, images, and other elements on a website to make it seem neat and professional by using custom frame layouts.

Activities

1. Discuss the Grid Types and Configurations
2. Discuss everything about Canva frames

CHAPTER FIVE

UNDERSTANDING TYPOGRAPHY AND TEXT

Including and Modifying Text

Adding text to Canva is an excellent way to familiarize yourself with its layout and design capabilities. The writing tool in design is located on the screen's left side.

Step One: Open the text tool

To add text, start with a blank canvas or open your design project. On the left side of Canva's interface is a toolbar with many options. When you locate the Text tab, click on it. **This will display three basic text choices in a window:**

- Include a Heading: For huge, eye-catching text, such primary headings or titles.
- Include a Subheading: A little bit smaller text that works well for supporting information or supplementary titles.
- Include a Body Text: For larger texts, such paragraphs or in-depth information.

One of these options may be selected by clicking on it, or you can click and drag the text type directly into your canvas.

Adding Text from Scratch in Step Two

To create a text box by hand, just click on the canvas and hit the "T" key on your computer. Without requiring any action on your part, this shortcut inserts a new text box in the center of the picture. You may write your own information directly to replace the default text that appears.

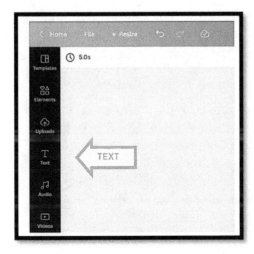

Changing Text in Canva

To modify a text box, double-click on it.

- Modify or remove its contents. To format your text, use the text edit options shown on the editor toolbar.
- To complete, click outside the text box.

Selecting a Font

- From the toolbar, choose the font dropdown.
- Locate or choose the typeface you want to use.

Footnote: An additional 5,000 typefaces are available to you if you have a Canva Pro membership. This makes it simple to locate typefaces that aren't being used by anybody else.

Size of Text

- To change the font size, click on it and enter the new size. Additionally, you may enlarge or reduce the area by clicking on the plus or minus marks.

Color of Text

- To choose a different color from the color panel, click Text Color.

Textual emphasis

+ To highlight text, choose Bold, Italics, or Underline. If these icons are grayed out, it indicates that emphasis can't be added with the typeface currently in use.

Alignment of Text

+ Click Center, Left, Right, or Justify repeatedly until the desired arrangement is selected.

The List

+ Click Bullet List to turn your text into a list of bullets.
+ Click the Bullet list icon once again to add your content to a list with numbers. The bullets will become numbers as a result.

Spacing of Text

+ Press the text spacing button.
+ Adjust the line and letter spacing sliders to the desired value.

Pairing Fonts

Let's imagine your brand is well-designed, has a vibrant color palette, and conveys clear messaging. It reminds me of Comic Sans and Papyrus. Indeed? That's the magic—or lack thereof—of assembling typefaces. They serve as the voice of your brand, whispering your personality, making your writing simpler to read, and guiding readers through your content as a kind of helpful guide. A crisp headline with attention-grabbing serifs may be followed by gentle content devoid of serifs. You may communicate with it and see it in a manner that highlights the key details without making your eyes water. Look at the identical statement in all capital letters, printed in Comic Sans. It would seem disorganized. Fonts are what give a brand a "wow" or "whoa, back up!" effect, friends. Instead of arguing about style, let's harness the power of font pairings!

Recognizing the Fundamentals of Font Pairing

Creating visually appealing font combinations is a major component of graphic design. You must understand the fundamentals of font matching, including how to line, balance, and contrast typefaces, in order to do this.

These concepts may be deconstructed as follows:
- **Contrast:** This element of font matching is crucial since it gives your design a balanced and intriguing appearance. You may create a wide variety of appearances by combining fonts with various styles, such as serif and sans-serif fonts, bold display fonts, and regular fonts.
- **Balance:** It's also critical to ensure that your design's components are arranged correctly and present well. This is another crucial guideline for the ideal Canva font pairings. Make the necessary adjustments to the fonts' size, weight, and scale to ensure that they complement one another.

The degree to which the styles you're matching read and appear well together is known as compatibility. To ensure that everything works together, you should consider your design's general tone and message in addition to the particular styles you're utilizing. If you understand and adhere to these guidelines, you may combine typefaces in ways that improve the design, make them simpler to read, and look nice. Don't be scared to defy the "rules" if you've found a suitable font combination. You'll become quite skilled at arranging typefaces in visually appealing ways as you improve.

The Most Ingenious Font Combinations on Canva

Lovelo & Gistesy

Lovelo is a bold, contemporary style that boosts self-esteem. For titles and headlines, this technique is quite effective. When combined with the elegant and sophisticated script typeface Gistesy, it takes on a completely distinct appearance. Gistesy's flowing curves and Lovelo's strong lines combine to create designs that are more sophisticated and captivating. This combination might be utilized to create visually striking social media visuals or brand items.

Le Jour Serif & Hero Light

LE JOUR SERIF
Hero Light

Le Jour Serif is a sans serif typeface that looks beautiful for a long period. It looks nice in many various design styles because to its clean lines and versatility. Hero Light is a straightforward sans-serif typeface that complements it well for a chic and contemporary appearance. Hero Light is a straightforward typeface that complements Le Jour Serif's timeless design. They both complement one other effectively for blogs or news articles.

Quiche Bold & Poppins

Quiche Bold
Poppins

If you're looking for something chic and contemporary, Quiche Bold is a terrific design to consider. Its powerful geometric features make it suitable for large headings and messaging. Quiche Bold's appearance is enhanced when used with Poppins, a versatile sans-serif typeface. This combination is excellent for product boxes, presentations, and brochures since it makes your designs seem polished and easy to read.

Versailles & Open sans Light

VERSAILLES
Open Sans Light

Wearing Versailles with Open Sans Light will make you seem sophisticated and well-groomed. Versailles' ornate lettering gives you a sense of wealth and prosperity. This contrasts well with the bright and clean design of Open Sans bright, which makes it simple to read and visually appealing. High-end business cards, wedding invites, and event signage look fantastic with that combination.

Lemon Tuesday & Aileron Thin

Lemon Tuesday is an excellent option as well. You may use its bright and enjoyable mood into your creations. It's so adorable that it seems to have been handmade. Because it highlights the text's hue, Aileron Thin, a thin, light sans-serif font, complements Lemon Tuesday. Together, these two look fantastic in children's novels, on this entertaining social media post, or in imaginative branding materials.

Putting Canva Font Pairings into Practice

It's time to include these beautiful Canva font combinations into your work now that you are aware of them. **The following advice will help you make the most of these sets:**
- Preserve visual harmony: Make sure the font pairings you choose complement the design's general tone and subject in order to keep it appearing nice.
- Take hierarchy into account: To create a distinct visual order, use a variety of font sizes, weights, and styles. What the reader needs to see will be clearly visible.
- Try new ideas and keep trying them out by iterating and experimenting. Don't be scared to experiment with different fonts and styles. To determine which combination works best for your design, you may experiment.
- Remain consistent: To give your design a cohesive, expert appearance, employ the font combination you've chosen throughout.

You may use these font sets to elevate your Canva creativity and design abilities to a whole new level.

Examining Other Font Combinations

In addition to the previously mentioned combinations, Canva offers a vast array of typefaces for you to experiment with. Consider a number of distinct pairings. Look at more pairings that fit your project requirements and style. You may be surprised by the combinations that fit your design objectives.

Text Styles and Effects

Using Text Effects

On Canva, there are several methods to add effects to text. The Format menu's Text Format choices or the Text tool may be used to apply effects to text. Click "Effects" in the toolbar after selecting the text you want to modify to see the text effects. Style effects and form effects are the two categories on the left. We'll start by looking at the stylistic affects. With these awesome word effects, let's have some fun. We'll discuss the functions of the styles as we move through them.

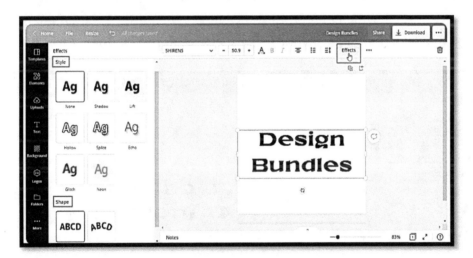

Shadow

It gives the impression that your words are shadowed. You may alter the shadow's appearance in a few ways. To fine-tune each parameter, turn the knobs to the left or right. The choices that are shown are appropriate. To alter the distance between the shadow and the text, adjust offset. The direction might alter the shadow's path based on the words. You may adjust the transparency and blur for each shade to alter how see-through the shadow appears. We can also alter the color of the shadow by clicking on the color tile below and choosing the preferred hue from the design box on the left.

Elevate

This effect gives the impression that your text is being dragged off the page. This effect just allows you to alter the strength of the shadow behind the lettering. By shifting the tool to the right, you may intensify the fuzzy shade. Shifting it to the left will weaken it.

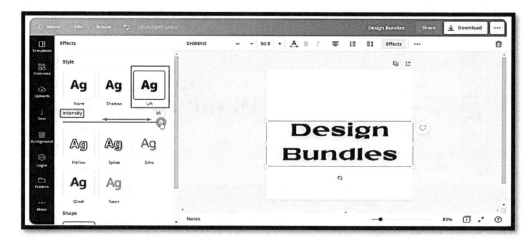

Hollow

This effect makes your text stand out by smoothing out the characters. Thick, not thin, styles are the most effective. You may adjust the thickness of your form with the width tool.

You may also use the hollow effect to smooth out the borders of your text. You should start with a decent text if you want to create one. To see further options, click the three dots on the toolbar. Then, to create a duplicate of your text, click the copy button. Click on the color tile and choose a color from the list on the left to alter the contrast of your original text.

Select the second word, which ought to be dark. Next, choose Hollow from the selection on the left under Effects. Overlay the heavy text with the outline text.

Splice

Splice, the following effect, combines the shadow and emptiness effects. To change the appearance of your split text, you simply slide the control bar four times. The direction of the shadow text behind the outline text, the thickness of the text outline, and the distance the shadow departs from the text outline may all be altered. By clicking on the color tile below and selecting your preferred color from the editing panel on the left, you can also alter the color of the shadow text.

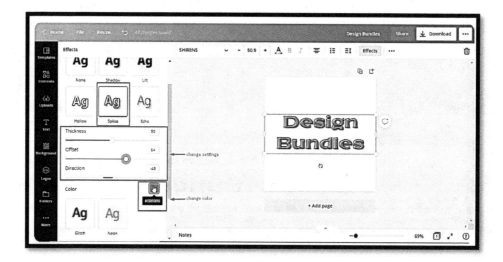

Echo

Echo creates the illusion that your text is piled by copying it twice and placing it behind one another. Changes may be made via color, offset, and direction. The distance between the main text and the shadow text is altered by offset. The shadow text shifts in various ways behind the main text. Additionally, the color alters the color of the shadow text. When the text is neither too thick nor too thin, it is easier to see.

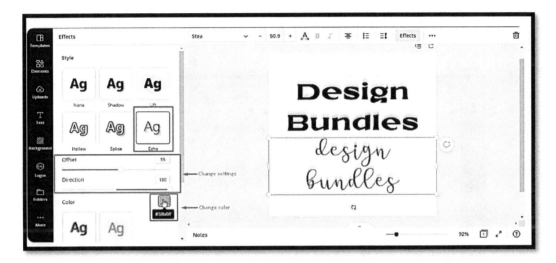

A glitch

The "glitch" effect will give the impression that your text is not aligned correctly. Changes may be made via color, offset, and direction. Color modifies the color of the glitch, whereas Gap modifies the size of the gap. Electric cyan, light neon pink, neon blue, and brilliant red are the only colors you can glitch in. The glitch effect looks excellent on both thin and thick letters.

The Neon

The vivid glow of the neon effect gives your text the appearance of being from the 1980s. This effect just allows you to adjust the neon glow's intensity. Moving the tool to the left increases the light but decreases the clarity of the text. The lettering is readable and the light is weaker as it is moved to the right.

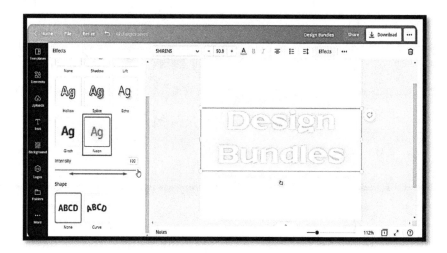

The curve

All of the style effects are finished. Curve text, which we'll discuss next, is the sole shape effect. Text may be curved with Curve. You may adjust the curve's strength by moving the curve tool to the right. It enables you to make a complete or half circle out of your text.

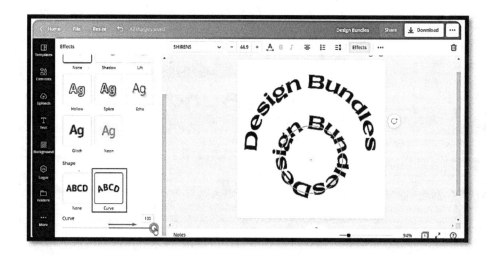

By moving the curve tool to the left, you may alter the curve's angle in a new method.

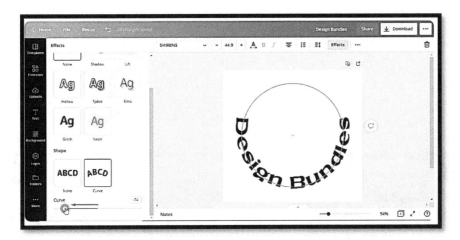

Finally, keep in mind that although any of the Canva text effects may help your text stand out, you should only utilize a small number of them in your design. Additionally, keep in mind that they only appear well in title texts—not body texts.

Pro Tip: After applying effects to the text in Canva, you may not be able to read it.

Options for Text Alignment

Pro Tip: If you're not cautious, it's simple to line things up incorrectly with Canva. You may always utilize the alignment tools to correct any misaligned objects. But you may produce a poor plan if you don't know how to utilize the positioning tools. The toolbar's text alignment buttons are the initial method for aligning text. Click one of the "Align" buttons after selecting the words you want to match. You have the option to justify, center, right, or left align.

Text may be fixed in another method. Make use of the Text Properties menu's options. Double-click the word you want to align, or click the "T" icon in the toolbar. The menu will appear as a result. Next, click "Alignment" in the Text Properties menu, and from the drop-down menu that displays, choose the alignment technique you like. Using the Format Menu's alignment options is the third method for aligning text. Click the "Format" tab at the top of the Canva Designer to access this page. Next, go to the Format Menu and choose "Text alignment". Select the desired alignment type by clicking on the drop-down menu next to it.

There is a fourth method for aligning text in HTML code. This may be accomplished by appending the values "align=left", "align=center", "align=right", or "align=justify" to the text's beginning tag. It's as simple as that! Canva allows you to arrange text in four distinct ways. If you need more assistance using Canva, contact our support staff or visit our Help Center.

Activities

1. Explain the process of including and Modifying Text
2. Explain the Most Ingenious Font Combinations on Canva
3. What are the several methods to add effects to text?

CHAPTER SIX

UTILIZING GRAPHICS AND IMAGES

Adding Your Own Images

Actions to take are as follow:

- Visit www.canva.com and log in to your Canva account to access your account. Once logged in, choose or start a design project.
- **Find the Uploads Tab:** The toolbar of the design editor has the Uploads tab on the left. You may control the images, videos, and audio snippets you share in this area.
- **Select "Upload Files":** Select "Upload Files" from the menu. You can find this under the Uploads tab. In the file explorer window that appears, you may search your computer for the photo or pictures you want to share.
- **Choose Your Image(s):** Select one or more images from your tablet or phone, then click Open (or a comparable button, depending on your operating system). Numerous image file formats, including JPEG, PNG, and SVG, are compatible with Canva.
- **Await Upload Completion:** The Uploads tab will display the images you uploaded. There will be a progress bar shown while the file is being uploaded. You may see the picture when the procedure is complete.
- **Drag and Drop onto the Canvas:** After the image has been posted, you may drag it directly into your painting from the Uploads tab. If necessary, you may adjust the image's size, location, and other parameters.

Using the Canva mobile app to upload images

To use the Canva mobile app to upload images:

- **Open the Canva App:** Open the Canva app on your tablet or smartphone, then log in with your credentials.
- Tap the Plus icon at the bottom of the screen after opening your design project to access the Uploads Section. Choose Uploads from the available choices.
- **Upload Files from Your Device:** Select pictures from your device's gallery, file manager, or cloud storage by tapping the Upload Media button.
- **Add Images to Your Design:** The picture will be saved in the Uploads area when it has been posted. To add the picture to your canvas and alter it as you see fit, tap on it.

Personalizing Uploaded Pictures

Canva provides you with a wealth of tools to enhance your photos and incorporate them into your design once you've uploaded them.

Positioning and Resizing

- **Resize:** Use the handles on the corners of the image to adjust its size. To make the image larger or smaller, you may drag it in or out.
- **Repositioning:** Click and drag the image to move it around the board. Alignment instructions will appear to assist you in positioning it correctly.

Cropping

- **Crop Tool:** Double-click the image or choose "crop" from the toolbar. You may move the cropping handles to highlight the desired area of the image.

Adjustments and Filters

- You may adjust brightness, contrast, and saturation directly or use one of Canva's pre-made filters to alter the atmosphere of your image.
- To get a polished or creative appearance, try experimenting with effects like vignettes or tints.

Transparency

- To change the opacity of your image, use the transparency slider. This may be used to create subtle backdrops or overlay photos on top of other elements.

Shapes and Frames

You may create your own cutouts or fit the recently uploaded image into certain patterns by dragging it into a frame or shape from the Elements page.

Canva Pro's Background Removal feature

With a single click, Canva Pro's background removal tool eliminates the backdrop, allowing you to concentrate on the image's topic. This feature is excellent for creating product or profile photos.

Handling Uploaded Pictures

Canva's Uploads page arranges your uploaded images so you can quickly locate and use them for various purposes. **Here are a few strategies for managing your files:**

 - **File Organization:** To maintain your library neat and user-friendly, remove uploads that are unnecessary.
 - **Reuse Images:** A picture that you share remains in your account and may be used in other designs without requiring a new upload.
 - **Folders (Canva Pro Feature):** To make your shared images easier to locate, organize them into folders. This is particularly helpful for businesses or organizations that manage several assets.

Advice for Improving Uploaded Pictures

 - **Select High-Quality photographs:** When uploading photographs, make sure they are of a high caliber to ensure that they seem crisp and professional, particularly for printed designs.
 - **Compress Large Files:** Reduce the size of large photo files without sacrificing quality to prevent files from uploading slowly. You may reduce the size of files before sharing them by using programs like TinyPNG.
 - **Use Transparent Backgrounds (PNG):** Use a PNG file with a transparent backdrop if you require an image without a background, such as an icon or logo.
 - **Respect Copyrights:** Verify that you have the legal authority to distribute any images before doing so. Information that is protected by copyright should not be used unless you are the owner or have permission from the owner.

Typical Problems and Solutions

 - **Slow Uploads:** Check your internet connection if you're experiencing issues uploading. Reducing the file size might also be beneficial.
 - **File Types Not Supported:** In general, Canva supports image files such as JPEG, PNG, and SVG. If your file isn't uploading, make sure it belongs to one of these categories.
 - **Picture Distortion:** A picture may not be crisp enough for the size you wish to utilize it in if it seems to be composed entirely of pixels. Switch it to a higher-resolution file.

Using the Photo Library on Canva

Canva's photo library is a vast selection of excellent images that you can use to improve your designs. With the use of this function, users may access millions of images for a wide range of uses, including marketing campaigns, corporate branding, instructional resources, and personal projects. Because the picture collection is integrated into Canva's interface, it's simple to locate, choose, and edit images that suit your imaginative vision. You may save time by not having to search for photos on other websites and improve the appearance of your designs if you know how to utilize Canva's picture collection.

Getting into the Photo Library on Canva

The photo library is often located under the Photos tab on the left-hand toolbar when using Canva's design editor. This section has a carefully selected selection of stock images arranged by topic, style, and subject. Whether you're searching for images of people, cuisine, landscapes, abstract patterns, or business-related subjects, the library provides a wide variety of images to suit your requirements. To access the library, just choose the Photos tab. From here, you may search by keyword, browse through popular groups, or apply filters to focus your search. Canva's image collection offers both free and premium photos. A crown symbol indicates paid photographs. With a Canva Pro membership, you may access premium images, or you can pay a nominal amount for each one.

Choosing the Correct Picture

Search Features

One of the greatest approaches to locate the ideal image fast is to use the search bar located in the Photos tab. Enter keywords that best characterize your search, such as "mountains," "office desk," or "summer vibes." Canva's intelligent search algorithm will then provide results that fit your query, often along with suggestions to help you make a more focused selection. In addition to "beach," the library may also recommend "sunset beach," "tropical beach," or "beach activities." This is a useful tool to have if you're unsure on the kind of image you want to use for a trip blog.

Examining Types

Finding images that match the concept of your project is made simple by Canva's grouping of its photo collection. Nature, technology, business, education, fashion, and way of life are some of the most popular categories. You may locate images that complement your design's attitude and goal by browsing through these groupings.

Options for Filtering

You may use Canva's screening features to refine your search results by:
- **Color:** Select a color filter to align photos with your design's color palette.
- **Orientation:** You may choose between square, portrait, or landscape orientations depending on your design's layout.
- **Image Type:** You may limit the results to just display drawings or photos based on your needs.

By using filters, you may rapidly identify the most pertinent images without having to go through irrelevant stuff.

Including Images in Your Design

To include an image from Canva's collection into your design, just click or drag it into the canvas. **Even though the picture will automatically match the arrangement, you may still alter its placement, size, and overall appearance.**
- **Placement:** To move the image about the board once you've placed it where you want it, click and drag. To assist you center or align the picture with other elements of your design, Canva's alignment suggestions will appear.
- **Resizing:** By sliding the image's sides, you may adjust its size. Unless you intentionally crop or damage the image, Canva ensures that the aspect ratio remains constant.
- **Cropping:** If the image includes sections that are unnecessary or has to fit within a certain frame, use Canva's crop tool. Double-clicking the image or using the toolbar's crop tool will alter the visible portion.

Making Use of Grids and Frames

Canva's frames and grids are excellent for incorporating images into neat layouts. A photograph will remain in place on its own if you drag it into a frame or grid. When creating collages, mood boards, or designs with several images, this is really useful.

Editing Pictures

Canva's photo collection offers more than simply images; it also offers tools for enhancing and altering them to match the aesthetic of your project. You may use these methods to transform a stock photo into a distinctive visual element that complements your artistic vision.

Filters

With Canva's built-in filters and design, you can rapidly alter the mood or tone of a picture. For instance:

- To make your picture seem warm and welcoming, use a warm filter.
- For a vintage or dramatic look, use a black-and-white filter.
- To draw emphasis to colors, use high contrast filters.

Manual Modifications

For more control, Canva offers options for manual editing. You can alter items like:

- **Brightness:** Adjust the image's perceived brightness.
- **Contrast:** To add interest to the image, enhance the contrast between the bright and dark areas.
- **Saturation:** Colors may become brighter or less vivid by adjusting the saturation.
- **Blur:** Use a soft-focus effect to highlight certain areas of a picture or give depth.

Transparency

Changing a photo's transparency might help it blend in better with your design. This tool is quite useful for creating overlays and backdrops.

Photographic Effects

Canva Pro users may apply more intricate effects to their images, such as

- **Backdrop Remover:** This tool allows you to remove an image's backdrop with a single click, revealing simply the subject for usage in many design contexts.
- **Duotone:** Use a two-color overlay for a modern, creative appearance.
- **Vignette:** Use a gentle shadow around the edges to highlight the center of the image.

Including Images in Various Design Types

Canva's image collection is so adaptable that it may be used for a wide range of creative tasks:

- **Social Media Graphics:** Images may serve as the primary component of Pinterest pins, Instagram posts, and Facebook posts. To stand out in feeds that are already packed, choose images with plenty of color and contrast.
- **Marketing Materials:** For flyers, brochures, and posters, use images that highlight your message. You can connect with your audience and make your argument more effectively if you use the correct image.

- **Presentations:** To create visually appealing presentations, use high-quality images on your slides. Select images that support your arguments without detracting from the text.
- **Personal Projects:** Using images from the collection, you may create photo collages, birthday cards, and invitations. You may improve the overall appearance of the design by using ornamental or related images.

Image Editing: Adjustments, Cropping, and Filters

Additionally, Canva's photo editing tool is highly user-friendly and powerful. Compared to other picture editing programs, it offers a lot more capabilities. I'll walk you through using Canva's picture builder to create visually striking images.

How to Use Canva to Crop, Resize, and Flip Images

Let's start by examining how to upload your image to Canva's editor so you can begin editing it.

Step one: Go to Canva on your web browser to get started. When you click the "Create a design" button, a menu will appear. Select "Edit photo."

Step two: Select the Edit photo option after uploading the picture from your computer.

Step three: A project window will appear after your photo has been uploaded. You may now alter it using Canva's image editor.

Canva's Crop Images

Cropping allows you to concentrate on the image's primary topic by removing unnecessary portions. To crop out a photo, select it in the project window and click the Crop button at the top.

Next, crop the image by altering the frame around it. Finally, click "Done" to save the modifications.

In addition, you may use the Elements tab to trim photos into shapes.

Resize Pictures in Canva

In Canva, you may adjust the size of your image to a certain size in addition to cropping it. Click the "Resize" icon in the upper left corner. Next, under "Custom size," enter the desired width and height.

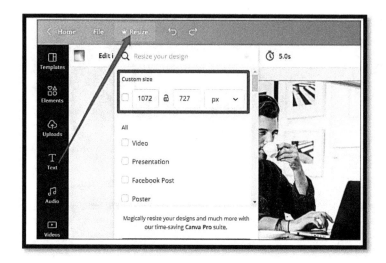

Canva's Flip Images

To see images from a new perspective, you may also flip them in Canva's image editor. Select the image in the project window and use the Flip button to change its orientation to either vertical or horizontal.

How to Use Canva Filters

Canva has several unique effects you can use to your photographs in addition to basic editing capabilities. **How to accomplish it.**

Step one: Select the image you want to modify in the photo editor, and then click the Edit Image button.

Step two: In the menu that appears on the left, scroll down to the Filters section. Any filter may be applied by clicking on it. Double-clicking on the filter will also modify its strength.

Alternatively, you may manually enhance the image using a few correction tools. To do that, choose the Adjust section after clicking the Edit picture icon in the top left corner. Click the "See all" button next to it to enlarge it.

You may manually adjust color, contrast, saturation, sharpness, and other aspects of your image to make it more captivating.

How to Use Canva to Remove the Background from an Image

To remove the background from a photo, you no longer need a brush and an eraser. Canva makes it simple to remove the backdrop from your photo with a few clicks. Click the Edit picture option at the top after selecting the backdrop you want to remove. Select the Background Remover option from the list.

The backdrop will disappear as a result.

71

To add interest to your image after it has been removed, you may add lettering and other features.

How to Use Canva to Add Text and Elements

You can crop and apply filters to a picture using any photo editing program, but Canva is unique in that it offers a vast collection of components and text styles that you can use to give your images a more polished appearance.

Include Details in the Image

Step one: To begin, choose the "Elements" option on the left, where you can see all of Canva's stickers, graphics, images, charts, and other content.

Step two: Click on the element to include it in your image. After adding the component, you may move, resize, and crop it using the toolbar above.

To avoid accidentally moving the additional element, you may also lock it. Click the lock symbol in the top right corner after selecting the item you want to lock.

You may remove an element by clicking the trash symbol next to it.

How to Get Edited Pictures

Once you've finished altering your photo, you'll need to download it. To download it, follow the instructions below. Click "Download" in the upper right corner, and then choose the desired format from the drop-down option under "File type." Finally, click "Download" to download your image.

Use Canva Web to crop an image into a shape

Here's how to transform an image into a shape using Canva on your computer browser.

Step one: To begin, click the Elements tab on the left. Select your preferred form by tapping "See All" after scrolling down to "Frames." The chosen form of the frame will be included into the design.

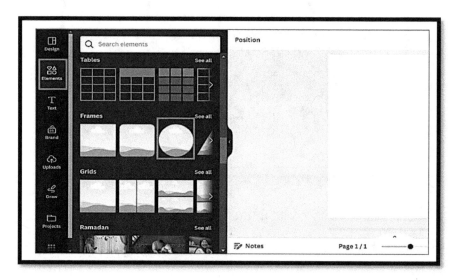

Step two: Select the frame, and then select the Uploads option located on the left. Drag and drop a picture into the frame to upload it. At this point, the image will take on the frame's form. You may drag the four corners to enlarge it. Double-clicking the image will allow you to reposition it in the frame to suit your needs.

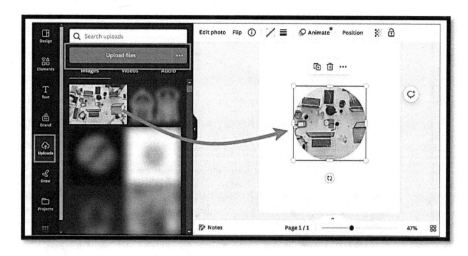

How to Use the Canva Mobile App to Crop an Image into a Shape

You may crop an image to a shape like this using the Canva software on your iPhone or Android device:

Step one: Launch Canva. Tap the "Elements" tab in the bottom bar, and then scroll down to "Frames." Tap "See All" and choose any form.

Step two: Your design will now include the frame. Add the picture you want to crop by tapping on Replace at the bottom.

Step three: At this point, the image will fit within the frame. You may drag the four corners to enlarge it. Double-tapping the image will allow you to move it within the frame until it fits.

By applying filters, creating animations, adding additional effects, or adjusting the transparency, you may further alter the cropped image.

How to Utilize Canva's Icons

Step one: Make a fresh design

Sign in by visiting Canva. Next, choose Create a Design from the menu in the top right corner. This will immediately provide a list of templates for usage. We'll use the Facebook Cover template. The new window that opens will be your workspace. Here, you may choose a design that complements your own style. To accomplish this, either put a word into the search field or click on a design in the panel on the left. I decided to use a Facebook cover design for finance. By selecting "See all," you may see the available covers for each category.

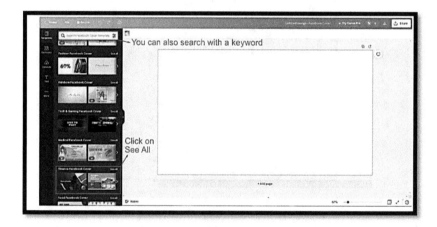

Some themes may display a little crown if you use Canva's free edition. These can only be used with the Canva Pro Version. Select the template you want to use by clicking on it on the left. Your screen is about to load this.

Step two: Give Canva your icons

Click the Upload Media button after selecting the Uploads symbol on the left side of the screen. Holding down Ctrl while clicking on several icons will select them all. I just posted PNG files, but you may publish SVG files as well. Choose the images you want, and then click "Open." You can alter the colors while working with SVG files, but not when working with PNG files. However, PNG files allow you to adjust Contrast, Brightness, and many other aspects. Your icons will now appear on the left side of the Uploads section.

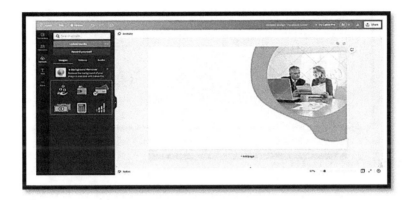

Step three: Utilize Canva's Uploaded Icons

To add an icon to your template, just click on it once it has been uploaded. Each time you click on an icon, it will be added.

Adjust Icon Size, Crop, and Position

Click and drag a corner handle in or out to adjust the size. The symbol may also be moved by clicking and dragging it. To crop the icon, click and drag the lines that go through the center of its top, bottom, and sides. The toolbar at the top of the screen also has the Crop option. The symbol will be surrounded by two boxes. The cropping box is the second, while the first is the original size. To change the crop size, click + drag, and then choose Done at the top.

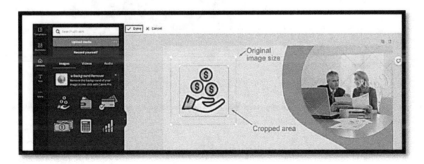

Flip the Icon Vertically or Horizontally

The ability to flip the picture either vertically or horizontally is also available on the top toolbar.

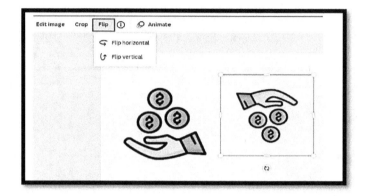

Modify the Icon Picture

A side panel with a number of editing options will emerge if you click on Edit picture at the top. You may also include your symbol in a mockup, like we did in the example picture below. That's awesome.

Simply click Edit Image once again to return to the icons you uploaded.

Options for Image Position

Use the Position options in the upper right corner to align the icons with the page.

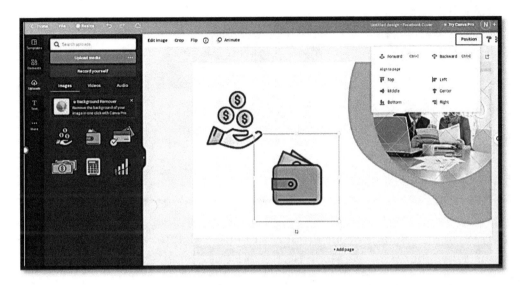

Moving a chosen icon forward (up one layer) or backward (down one layer) is possible here. This works particularly well for positioning an icon or picture beneath or on top of another image.

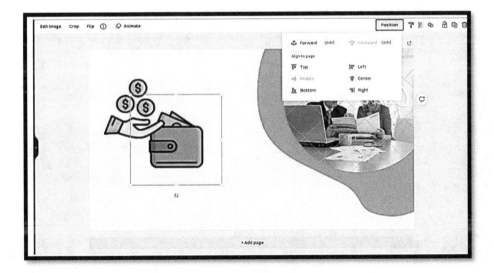

The Position menu will expand with more choices if you click on several icons. Here's where you can ensure that the icons are evenly spaced out using the Tidy up Feature.

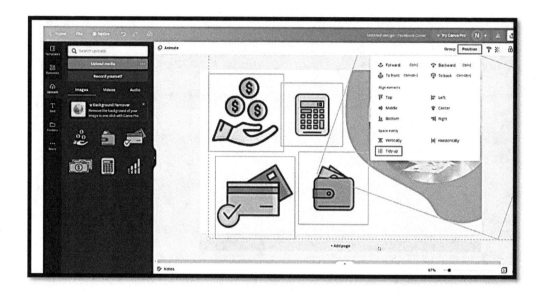

You may wish to arrange your photos together before adjusting their size and placement. When more than one icon is selected, this option is also available.

Extra Editing Choices

The Copy style is the next choice. This application allows you to copy and paste a format from one text or image to another. After changing the first icon in the image below, the Copy Style button was pressed. This style was then applied to the second icon.

The remaining choices consist of:
- **Transparency:** alter the icon's transparency
- **Link:** a place to include a hyperlink
- **Lock:** prevent editing of the icon.
- **Duplicate:** make a copy of the symbol
- **Delete:** remove the symbol.

Make the Icons Animated

Did you know that you could make the symbols move on Canva? This is your chance to have fun and create something that is unique. From the menu at the top, choose Animate. The animation options are located on the left. The selected symbol will move thanks to photo animations. When you utilize Page Animations, everything on the page will move. I used a program called Photo Animations. To get a brief overview of the options, move your mouse over them when an icon is chosen. To choose and add a picture, click on it. This will be saved as an MP4 when you choose Downloads. To get the most out of your icons, experiment with all of the options. The toolbar at the top will display the animation you selected. To remove the animation, choose Remove animation located in the lower left corner of the animate window.

To complete your template design, use Canva's text choices. To save your project, choose Share > Download. The last step is this. The version you're using will affect this option. You may alter the file type using the drop-down option, but keep in mind that I didn't include the motion, which is why the file type reads "PNG."

The file will have a watermark similar to the one below if you use the Free Version. Every time a Canva template is used, the watermark appears.

If you use Canva Pro, your design won't have the watermark. You can publish on social media using the Free Version, but the postings have a logo.

Activities

1. Explain the steps of using the Canva mobile app to upload images
2. Explain how to Use Canva to Add Text and Elements
3. Explain how to Use the Canva Mobile App to Crop an Image into a Shape
4. Explain how to Utilize Canva's Icons

CHAPTER SEVEN
DESIGN ASPECTS AND METHODS

Comprehending Layer Management

Before you can work with layers in Canva, you must organize your creative space. Each component has its own surface area, whether it is text, images, forms, or backdrops. To work with layers, follow these steps: Layers are layered like paper on top of one another. Whether layers are in what sequence determines whether sections appear in front of or behind other ones. You may move objects ahead or backward to alter the layers' order. Choose an item and use the toolbar or right-click menu to move it up or down in the stack. This will enable you to configure the levels. This gives you the ability to choose how they will seem and behave when they meet. By combining its components, you may make several things into a single entity. Because you can move or alter many components at once without having to adjust their placement, this makes it simpler to manage intricate designs. When locking layers, errors cannot be made. Although locked layers are still visible, you are unable to select or modify them until they are unlocked. This method of altering completed components protects them against unauthorized alteration. To concentrate on certain areas of your design or to temporarily clear your desk while working on other aspects of it, you may reveal or delete layers. Templates come with layers that are already configured to be easily changed. You may see and alter any element of the design, including the text, images, and colors, to suit your own preferences. You must understand how to utilize layers in Canva if you want to create designs that are cohesive and complement one another. Additionally, you have complete control over the placement and display of items in your compositions.

Identifying Canva Layers

   ↓ When you click on the design you want to work on in Canva Home's Recent Designs section, it should open.

- Select a design to work on first by clicking the "Create a design" button if you haven't already. Additionally, by selecting the "Custom size" option, you may create your own image.
- This stage should be skipped if you have a plan already. However, if you create a new one, you should start from scratch and save time by using one of the free templates in the Editor panel's Design panel.

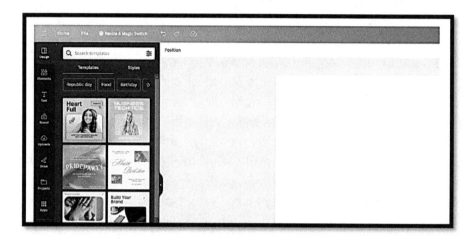

Once the design is complete, you may adjust the levels by going to the levels panel. There are many methods to do this. **By selecting the design with a right-click:**
- Locate the image and click on it to begin.
- After you've selected it, you may right-click on it to see further choices.
- Click Layer now, and then from the choice that appears, choose Show Layers.

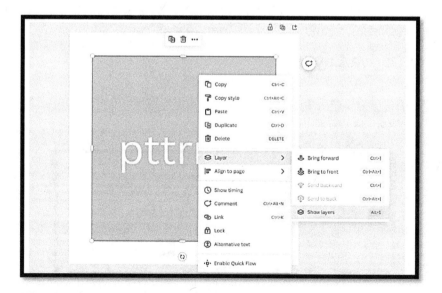

- The Layers panel ought to be on the left if you done it correctly.

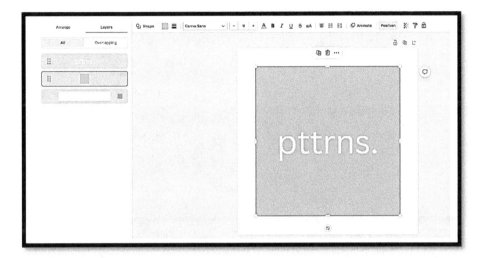

By selecting Position:
- Click on the design to choose it once you've placed it to the board.
- A list of possibilities will appear at the top as a result.
- From the list of alternatives, choose Position now. On the left will be the Arrange board.

- Click Layers to the right of Arrange to bring up the Layers panel.

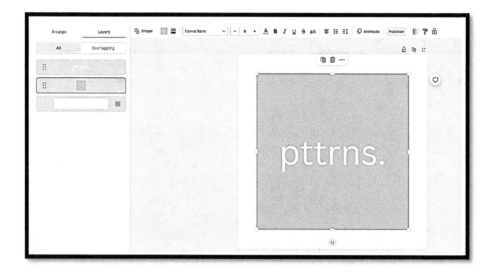

Advice: If you're working on a large plan, the aforementioned methods may take a while. They added the keyboard shortcut Alt + 1 to address this. Pressing this immediately brings up the Layers panel on the left.

Layer Organization in Canva

The levels panel makes setting up levels perhaps the simplest task. Here's how to arrange layers:

- In the Layers panel, click on the layer you want to reorder.
- To move a layer up or down the panel, click and hold on it.

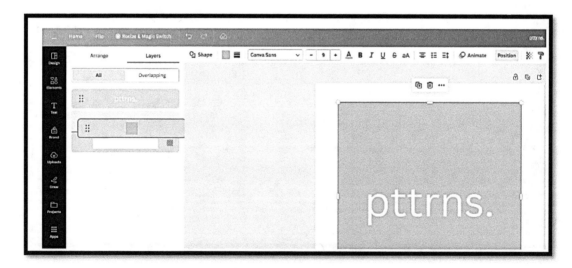

Advice: Changing each layer individually can take some time. It will be simpler if you click on multiple areas at once while holding down the Shift key. If you do it correctly, the layers will be selected and may be altered simultaneously.

Overlay Pictures

+ Go to Canva and enter your passwords to get started. Navigate to Recent Designs after visiting Canva Home. To begin working on a project, click on it.
+ Go to the main screen, choose "Create a design," and then pick a design to get started, if you haven't previously.
+ After loading the old or new design, choose Uploads from the Editor panel on the left. If you haven't already, click the Upload Files option, being careful to ensure that the file is background-free.

To start, click on the image to remove the backdrop. You may then click on the BG removal tool in the Effects panel that appears on the left after using the choices above to "Edit the image."

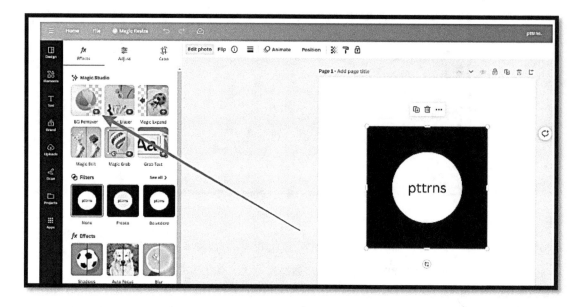

If you are unable to purchase Canva Pro, you may use free web tools such as remove.bg to eliminate the backdrop.

Canva Overlay Images: Illustration

Now that everything is prepared, you can begin placing the photo on top. Since the effects vary and may be utilized to create an endless number of designs, we created a basic example with steps that can serve as a starting point for all of them.

- Begin by giving the blank canvas a backdrop. It might be a design, text, image, or frame.
- Click on Uploads in the Editor panel now. Click on the image whose background you wish to include in the painting when the Uploads box appears.
- To see other possibilities for the picture's placement, right-click on the element at the top once it has been inserted. Depending on what you need to do, click Layer and then send to forward or backward.

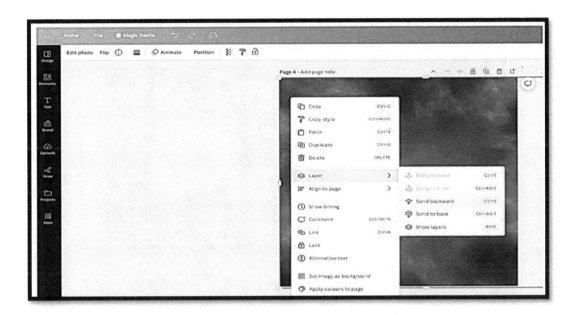

➕ Next, use the Transparency tool above the editor to adjust the transparency levels for the components. Next, use the scale to adjust the transparency of each image.

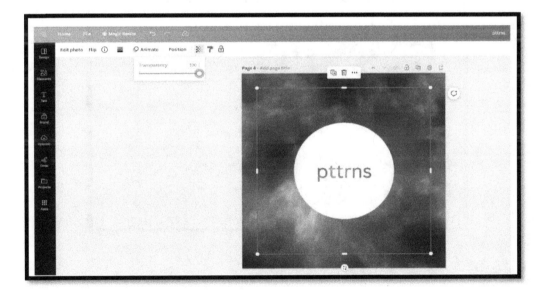

➕ Use unique styles and visual effects to enhance your design even more. You may choose elements from a vast collection of icons, vectors, and paintings if you like to develop your artistic concept further.

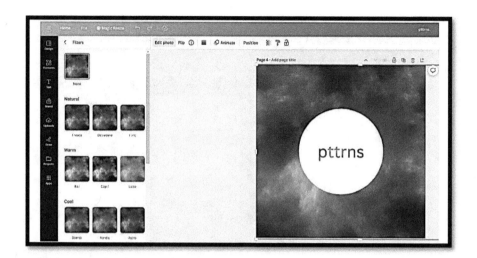

+ When you're finished editing, click Share in the upper right corner. From the options that appeared, choose Download. Next, choose the file type you want to download and click the "Download" option.

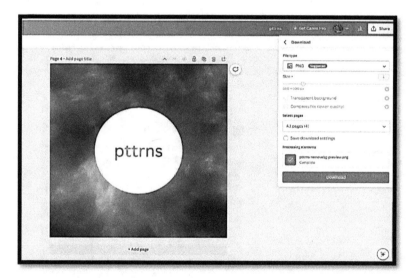

Using and Adapting Filters

Computer

+ To edit a photo or video, click on it.
+ Select Edit Photo or Edit Video from the editor's menu. On the side panel, you'll notice the photo editing choices that are given.
+ Click See All in the Filters section.

- Pick upon a filter to utilize it.
- Drag the Intensity scale underneath the filter you've selected to alter how powerful the filter is. The scale may be shifted to the left to make it weaker or to the right to make it stronger.
- To switch between filters, click on a different one.
- Selecting "None" will remove the applied filter.
- To save the modifications and end the filter row, click anywhere.

Mobile

- To modify an image or video, click on it.
- Select Filter from the editing toolbar below. To view it, you may need to swipe through the alternatives below.
- Select the one that you want to use. Swipe through the choices to see every setting.
- Select a filter to apply.
- To adjust the filter's strength, drag the intensity slider under the selected filter. The scale may be shifted to the left to make it weaker or to the right to make it stronger.
- To move between filters, tap on a different one.
- Selecting "None" will remove the applied filter.
- To save and exit the filter table, press on any location.

Advanced Methods for Canva Filters

Applying Several Filters

The ability to apply many tints to a single image is one of Canva Effects' best features. With the help of these tools, you may create stunning and distinctive effects for your images. This might make your pictures more noticeable. Canva allows you to use one filter at a time. After adding the first filter, just click "Add Filter" to add another. You may repeat these one or more times until you get the desired outcome. Keep in mind that an image that has too many effects may seem phony and unappealing. Try out several blends until you discover the one that works best for you, and be cautious not to apply too many filters.

Making Personalized Filters

You can also create frames using Canva, which is another awesome method to add uniqueness to your images. First, apply the effects that you choose to utilize to your image. To create your filter, you'll need this. After making your selections, click "Adjust" to access the advanced scale. Here, you may adjust the configuration of each filter to get the desired effect. Click the "Save Filter" button to save your filter after you're finished creating it. From so on, you may save time and effort by applying the same color to additional images.

Using Transparency and Gradients

Establishing a Gradient

Once you've uploaded the desired image, locate the "Elements" option above the "Uploads" function and click it. To start the search, write "gradient" into the resulting search field and hit the Enter key on your keyboard.

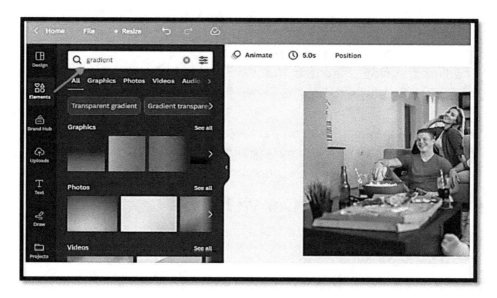

Canva offers a variety of color choices for you to choose from. Adding a color is simple; just browse the available options and choose the one you want. When you're finished working with the gradient, you may use your mouse or keyboard to click and hold on its corners. By moving the corners as you like, you may fill in the spaces. In the box located in the upper right corner of the screen, you may alter the image. If you are unable to locate the screen, click the "More" option to access it.

Reduce the transparency

You may adjust the strength of a gradient solid color to reduce its see-through. The color will seem thicker and harder as it becomes less transparent.

The correct response to "transparent gradient canva" is this. You may now choose a color. After selecting your option, click "Position" from the menu in the upper right corner of the program's screen.

To get the gradient where you want it, use the "backward" button to slide it back one layer at a time. You may need to click "backward" more than once to get the layers in the correct sequence. The gradient colors will appear when you click on them in the upper left corner of your Canva window. You may then choose your favorite color scheme.

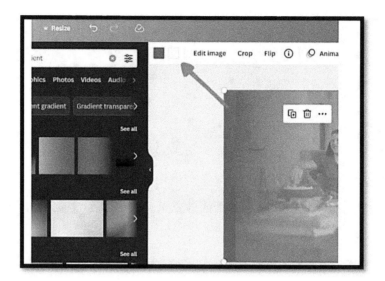

Once you have finished creating your photo, you must download it. You must locate the "Share" button, which is usually located in the upper-right corner of the screen, in order to do this.

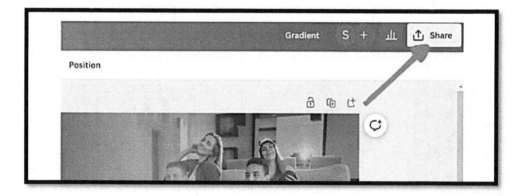

You will be prompted to choose a file to download when you click on it. The image will then be transferred to your smartphone.

How to Use Canva to Create a Gradient Text

- **Select "Create a Design."**
  - You must first create a unique gradient in Canva. After that, you may give the text a free gradient. You must manually choose the gradient colors and intensity levels if you want to utilize the tools included with Canvas.

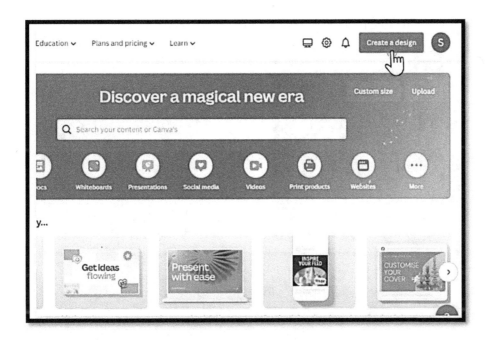

- Locate and press the "Create a design" button after logging in.
- **Navigate to the Element Option**
  - A menu bar or sidebar will then appear on the left.

- On this instance, locate and choose the "Elements" option on the tab. This will provide an inventory of all the many components that comprise the page.
- **Enter "Gradient" and choose a color.**
  - Next, enter "gradient" in the search field. Choose a free design after that.

- Locate the choices for two colors and choose one.
- **PNG file download**
  - Click "Save" and choose PNG as the file type to save your newly created file.
  - You can create a text effect now that you have a gradient.
- **Open a New Page**
  - Click the "Create new design" button to get to a new page.
  - You now have a blank area to work on.
- **Search for "Letter a frame" in Elements.**
  - Decide which aspects you want to focus on. After typing and selecting "Letter a frame," you may proceed.
  - Simply click on a letter while holding down the mouse button to choose it. Next, drag the letter to the desired location and release the mouse button.
  - You would have to follow the same steps for every letter you need.
- **Put Your Gradient File Here**
  - Insert the PNG file with your color. The gradient effect may then be added by dragging this file into each letter.

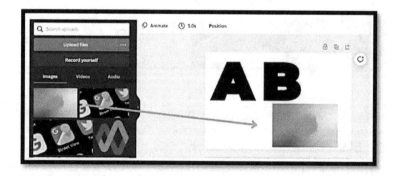

- Double-click on each letter to adjust its size so that the gradient picture extends to the page's boundaries.
- **Modify the Position**
  - The next step is to shift positions.

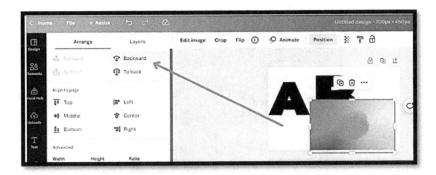

- Press the Position button in the top right corner after selecting the gradient, and then choose "Backward."

Use a Mobile Device to Create a Gradient in Canva on Text

You can now learn how to use Canva to add color to text on your phone.
- **Go to the Canva Dashboard:** To begin, simply go to the Canva homepage and locate the plus-sign-like button in the lower right corner of your screen. Clicking this button will lead you to other Canva sections where you may create new projects or designs.
- Select the "Post" option on Facebook.

➤ Kindly choose or click the "Facebook Post" template that appears.

✦ Navigate to the Type Gradient and Photos Option.

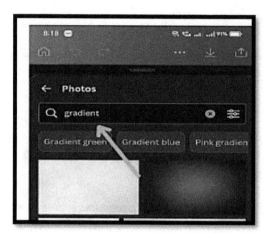

➤ To continue working on the task, click the "+" symbol one more time. A list of options ought to appear. To locate the appropriate images, choose "Photos" and then "Gradient." On Canva, locate the desired color image. Click on it to choose it after you've located it. Next, drag your gradient image to the whole template you're working with using your mouse or keyboard.

✦ **To add the text, choose the "Text" option:** Entering the words you wish the gradient to appear on is the next step. Put the text where you want the gradient effect to appear to accomplish this.

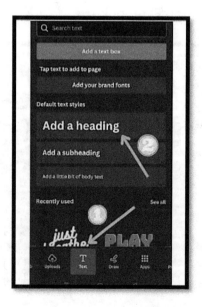

➢ When you see the "+" symbol, pick it up. Find the "Text" button now. A text editor window containing a few fonts and text styles will then appear. Select the text format you wish to use, such as a heading or a paragraph. Select a font from the current selection. Take your time and select the ideal font for your project from Canva's extensive selection. After selecting a typeface, add the text to the image. Next, adjust the text box's size by clicking and dragging its sides. In the text box, type the words you wish to use. Additionally, you are free to alter the structure however you see fit. Now you have a color and a font. The next step is to add color to the words.

♦ Modify the Text Color to Establish Transparency

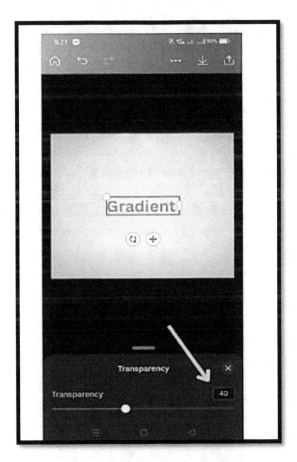

➢ Make the text white. Choose the text box and adjust the transparency level to 40% to alter the texts see-through.

♦ **PNG file download:** The image should be saved as a PNG file.

♦ Make a New Template on Canva

> Now build a fresh template that is blank.

+ **Upload a Fresh PNG File:** Find the PNG file you just produced in the "Uploads" section after tapping the "+" button and choose it. Use the "resize" option to make the PNG file the proper size when you're done uploading it.

+ **Remove Background**

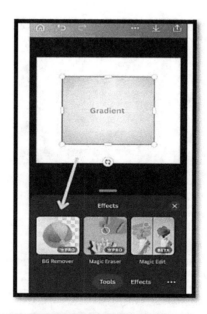

➢ Select "Effects" and then select "Background Remover." Give it some time to complete. You now know how to use Canva to alter the color of text on a white backdrop. You need to edit the language in the final few stages to make the pattern better.

➕ **Utilize the Adjust Feature and Crop Your Text**

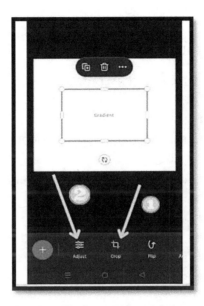

➢ You have to trim the text, click the "Adjust" option in the menu, then use the scales to modify the colors.

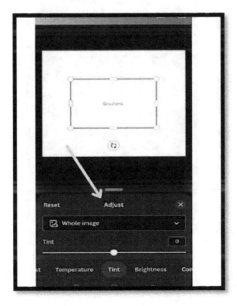

Create a Gradient Background with Canva

- Pick up the design you wish to use after choosing "Create Design." Pick out a YouTube clip template as an example.
- To discover gradient graphics, click on "elements" and type "gradient."
- To examine other alternatives and choose a preferred gradient, click "see all."
- Adjust the transition's size and color to match the overall image. If necessary, it is simple to reverse the pattern.

Create a Mobile Gradient Background

- **Press the "+" button.**
  - ➢ Locate the addition symbol (+) in the designer's lower left corner to create a gradient backdrop.
  - ➢ Simply press this button to add text, a gallery, or other elements to your project. The options are what you see.
- **Find the Background Option.**
  - ➢ To begin, swipe left and right till Background appears. Then, to change the backdrop, touch it. Swipe to access the "More" button if you are unable to locate it. The "Background" option should be included.

Below the search bar is the color tile. You must locate the component in order to alter its color. To utilize the color tile, just touch on it once you've located it. Swipe down on the area of the screen to return to your design. You may resume working on your project when this returns you to the main screen. By following these instructions, you may alter the gradient background's color.

- **Find the Icon for Palette:** Press the Palette button in Canva to access the color tools.

- ➢ A screen where you may choose a color or create your own will appear when you click here.
- **Press the "+" symbol.**
  - ➢ To open it, click the plus symbol (+).
  - ➢ This ought to provide you with a list of the colors that are now available.
- **Choose a New Color**
  - ➢ Click "Save" to save the newly selected color on your device. Additionally, you may click "Download" and choose the kind of file you want to get.

Use Canva to Create a Gradient Shape

- After selecting the template, click "Create a design."
- In the Elements section, search for "Gradient."
- Examine the graphs, and then choose "See All."
- You may choose from a variety of forms by selecting "Gradient Shape."

↓ Finally, adjust the gradient shapes' size to suit the whole image and apply magic as desired. If necessary, it is simple to reverse the pattern.

Comprehending Color Theory

Have you ever considered how painters and designers choose colors that complement one another? They are able to identify colors. In color theory, science and art may work together to help people choose complementary colors. In 1666, Isaac Newton created a circle with the color spectrum on it. The color wheel was created in this manner. Color theory is explained using a color wheel. It illustrates the relationship between colors. When two colors blend well together, it's called color balance. These are used by designers and artists to change the way things look or feel. By adhering to the guidelines for color pairing, you may use a color wheel to determine color balance. You may use color combinations to choose where to apply each hue to get visually appealing outcomes. There are two kinds of color wheels. The RYB (red, yellow, blue) color wheel is a constant tool used by artists to combine paint colors. Similar to a computer or television screen, the RGB color wheel blends colors. It is designed for internet usage. Since Canva is an online tool, its color wheel is an RGB wheel, which stands for "red, green, and blue."

Color Schemes

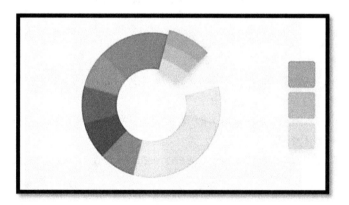

Monochromatic

The same basic hue comes in three distinct tints, tones, and shades. Comes in a gentle, timeless color combination. This color scheme complements one another and has a wide range of applications. Additionally, it's easy to utilize for design tasks.

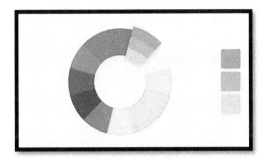

Analogous

On the color wheel, three hues are next to one another. This color palette works well in certain situations and is overpowering in others. Utilize the additional colors to highlight the primary color in a color scheme to improve its appearance.

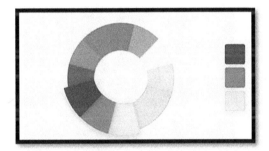

Triadic

On the color wheel, the three hues are present in equal proportions. These colors vary greatly from one another, yet not as much as the complimentary colors do. As a result, it may now be used in more situations. This combination creates vivid and striking color combinations.

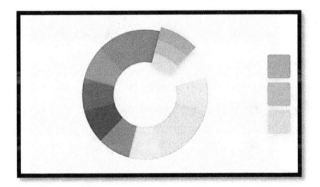

Complementary

Two colors on the color wheel that is not next to each other. The contrast and impact of these colors are powerful. When paired together, they will seem softer and stand out more.

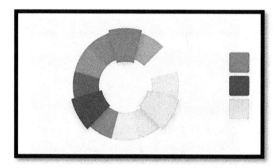

Triadic

On the color wheel, the three hues are present in equal proportions. These colors vary greatly from one another, yet not as much as the complimentary colors do. As a result, it may now be used in more situations. This combination creates vivid and striking color combinations.

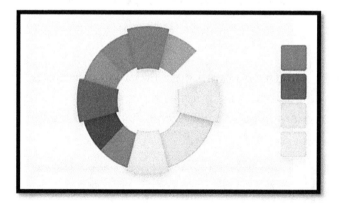

Tetradic

The four hues on the color wheel are separated by an equal amount of space. Make one color stand out in a tetradic color scheme and utilize the other colors to accentuate it. It is more difficult to maintain order when there are too many colors.

Colors: Primary, Secondary, and Tertiary

The wheel has twelve primary colors. The RGB color wheel is composed of the following colors: red, orange, yellow, green, spring green, cyan, azure, blue, violet, magenta, and rose. Primary, secondary, and tertiary are the three categories into which the color wheel may be divided.

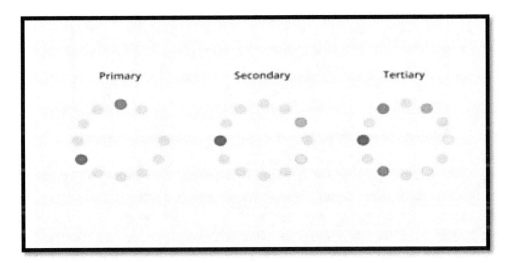

+ **Primary colors:** The primary colors on the RGB color wheel are those that combine to form white light. Shades of red, green, and blue are present.
  ➢ On the RYB color wheel, primary colors are those that are incompatible with other hues. The main hues are red, blue, and yellow.
+ When two primary colors are combined, **secondary colors** are produced. Three more hues are available. On the RGB wheel, these are the hues cyan, magenta, and yellow. Yellow light is produced when red and green are combined. Cyan light is the result of combining blue and green. Additionally, magenta light is produced when red and blue are combined.
  ➢ Purple is the result of combining red and blue. Red and yellow combine to form orange. Moreover, blue and yellow combine to form green.
+ **Tertiary colors:** Tertiary colors are created by combining primary and secondary colors. The tertiary hues are six in number. Blue, rose, chartreuse green, spring green, and chartreuse green are the hues that make up the RGB wheel.
  ➢ The RYB color wheel's tertiary hues are red-orange, yellow-orange, yellow-green, blue-green, blue-violet, and red-violet.

Cool and Warm Shades

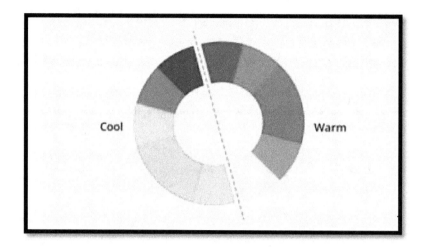

Cool and warm groups may also be distinguished on the color wheel. What other term is used to describe color temperature? It indicates a color's degree of warmth or coolness. Cool and warm hues are often well-balanced on a color wheel. According to color psychology, we experience a range of emotions depending on the color temperature. People claim that although chilly colors make people feel peaceful and alone, warm colors make them feel pleasant and energized. Warm tones fall between red and yellow. People claim that these hues give them a pleasant, sun-like feeling. Blue, green, and purple are examples of cool hues. People claim that these hues conjure images of cool objects, such as water.

Tone, tint, and shade

Shades, tints, and tones may be created by combining black, gray, and white with a base hue.
- **Shade:** To create a shade, combine black with a base color to make it darker. This makes it fuller and darker. A few of the hues are too vivid and intense.
- **Tint:** A base color and white are combined to create a tint. The hue becomes softer as a result. This may lessen the brightness of a color or improve the appearance of too bright color combinations.
- **Tone:** Combine a base hue with black and white (or gray) to create a tone. Tone variations of the primary hue are similar to shades. Tone colors may reveal depths that aren't immediately apparent from the base color and are less likely to seem light.

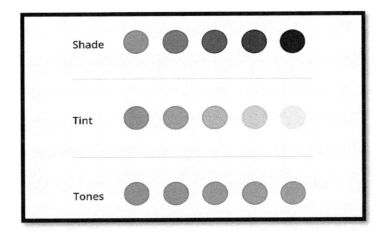

Luminance, Saturation, and Hue

- Any color on the color wheel is a hue. You may alter a color's brightness and saturation by using a color wheel or a color picker.
- A color's saturation level indicates how vivid or pure it is.
- A color's brightness is the amount of light or shine it contains.

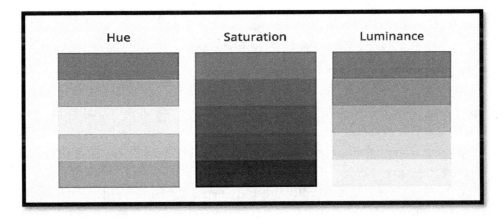

An overview of the Color Picker Tool

The "color picker" is a useful feature in Canva that allows you to alter the colors and appearance of design elements. Here is a summary of its capabilities and operation:

The Color Picker Tool's Access

Any color-based text, shapes, backdrops, or pictures may be altered with the color picker tool. All you need to do is click on the color tile in the menu next to it to alter the color.

The Potential of the Color Picker Tool

+ **Color Palette:** The color picker displays the most recent colors you've used in your work together with a list of basic colors. This makes it simple to keep on course while doing your duties.
+ **Custom Colors:** To create your own colors, click the "+" icon in the form of a rainbow. This launches a full-color picker where you may enter precise hex codes to get the desired color or adjust the hue, saturation, and brightness (HSB).
+ **Hex Codes and RGB Values:** If you are certain of the color you want, you may enter its hex code into the color picker. Instead, you may create your own hue by altering the RGB settings.
+ **Eyedropper Tool:** This tool allows you to import photos instantly or choose a color from anywhere in your design. This aids in precisely matching colors to other elements of an image or design.
+ **Brand Kit Integration:** The color selection is compatible with the Brand Kit tool if you have Canva Pro. Finding and using your brand colors is much easier as a result. This guarantees that anything bearing your name will have the same appearance.
+ **Transparency:** The color setting also includes a transparency number. This allows you to alter the degree of opaqueness of the color you have selected. This may assist you in creating effects with soft backgrounds, patterns, or several layers.

Using the Tool for Color Picking

+ **Step one:** To start, click on the item you want to highlight by altering its color. It will be surrounded by a box.
+ **Step two:** Select the color square in the top left corner by clicking on it. It will display the current color of the item you selected.
+ **Step three:** Click the box with the plus symbol in the center on the left. Now choose a different hue.

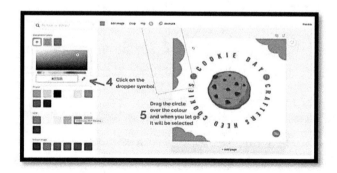

- **Step four:** When the drip symbol appears, click and hold on it. You can move around this circle that forms.
- **Step fifth:** Drag the circle over the design or the whole screen to choose the color. When you let go, the new color appears in the document color list on the left. The new color will also be applied to the item you first selected.

How to Use and Adjust Colors in Designs

Variations in Design Elements' Colors

- There is one item you would want to alter. Depending on how many colors the section you selected contains, one or more color tiles will appear on the menu above the editor.
- To alter a color, click on its tile. Along with other things, it will display the colors of your paper. It will also display the color schemes you have previously created.
- The element you selected will be colored with the color you clicked on in the color panel.
- Click the tile labeled "Add a new color" in the color box to alter the color. Drag the circle to choose a new color. The hex color code may be entered here. Slopes may also be used.
- Once you've clicked on the rainbow tile, drag your cursor over the section of your design that you wish to alter color and click the eyedropper icon. To add color, click on the section.

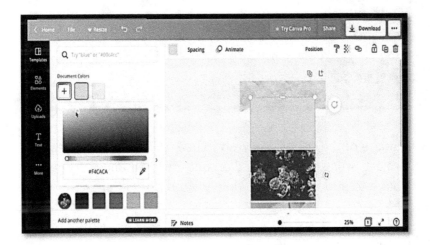

Keep in mind: Only the Canva computer program and Google Chrome and Edge support the eyedropper color choice.

With only one click, alter the color scheme of your Canva design

Step one: Pick a Template

+ If you don't currently have a project underway, you may browse Canva's collection on the homepage and choose a helpful template. Do you have a more detailed search in mind? You may use the search bar. After selecting your preferred template, click "Customize This Template."

Step two: Add Your Favorite Image

+ Even if a template has a color scheme, you may alter it as you want after you've selected it. If you are working on a complex project, you may want to utilize Canva's layers feature. Any minor color changes may wait till later; you don't have to worry about them now.

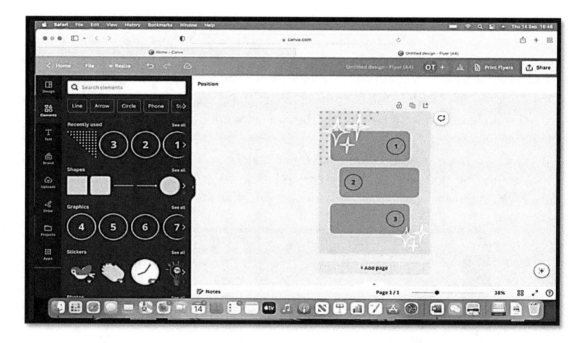

+ Add an image of the colors you wish to use to your existing design as soon as the whole project is finished. Simply drag and drop an image from your files into the project page to add it. From the Uploads tab on the left, you may also choose an older file.

Step three: Put Your New Colors to Use

Right-click on the image you want to use as a reference for the color scheme. Following that, choose "Apply colors to page." Your design should immediately include the picture's updated color scheme.

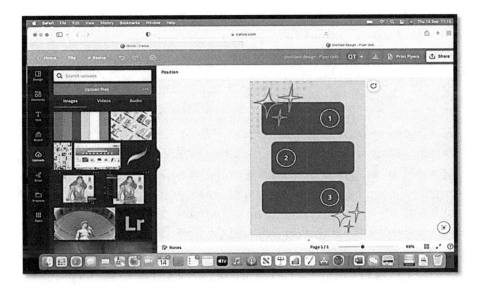

Anything that can be altered in Canva may be done so using this tool. Canva comes with a variety of built-in components that you may choose from. Additionally, you may utilize third-party tools like Adobe Illustrator to create color-changeable objects.

How to Prevent Canva Designs from Being Blurry

↓ Select the Appropriate Canvas Size

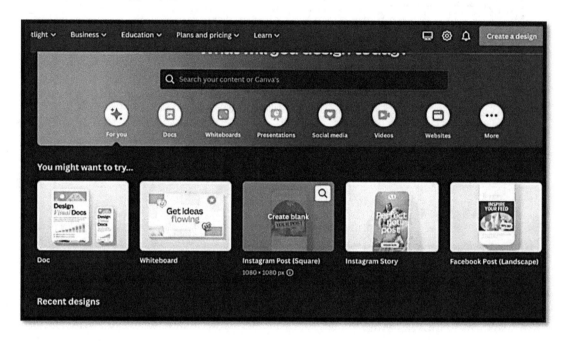

Once you start using Canva, you immediately discover that there are many sorts of canvas, each with a distinct size. Before you can utilize the canvas, you must specify its width and height. However, you can't choose any board. It must be the proper size, regardless of whether you create your own board or utilize one that is currently available. If it's not, your design will be hazy. In particular, don't utilize any lower-than-recommended amounts. An Instagram post, which has 1080 x 1080 pixels, is one example. Downloading and sharing a 400 × 400 px Instagram post will make it less visible. Uncertain about the appropriate paper size? Before you do something, be sure you know it; you can always check it up. Additionally, altering the design's size might make it seem hazy. Keep in mind that this is only possible for Canva Pro customers since the free edition does not allow you to alter the size of an image. If you complete a design and then feel it's too little, you may use Canva Pro to enlarge it. This is among the justifications for using Canva Pro.

↓ **Get Your Designs in PNG Format:** Both Instagram and Facebook reduce the size of images, which might give them a blurry appearance. Even if your drawings include text, this won't occur if they are saved as PNG files.

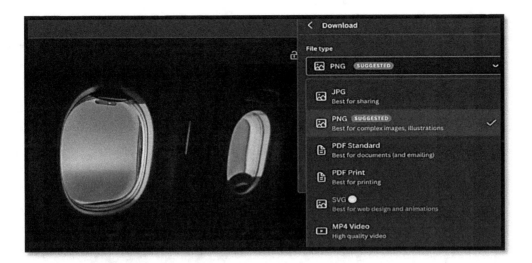

How to accomplish it:

➢ Click the "Share" button.
➢ Select "Download."
➢ From the list of file formats, choose PNG.
➢ After selecting the pages you want to download, click Download.

After that, a PNG file of your photo ought to be saved to your phone.

⊥ **Convert your designs after downloading them as PDFs:** If saving your drawings as PNGs doesn't work, you may save them as PDFs first, and then make the necessary changes. When you use a lot of pictures in your design, this is very helpful because it keeps the pictures clear. Select PDF Print over PDF Standard when saving your work as a PDF. If you want to print your photos, be sure they are high enough quality.

➢ Select PDF Print as the file format under Share > Download to preserve your work. Once you've saved it, you may go online and convert it to a PNG or JPG file.
🔸 **Don't Make Your Design Elements Too Big:** If necessary, you may adjust the size of your design elements while using Canva. Things like images and graphics may seem blurry if you expand them excessively.
🔸 **Adhere to High-Quality Pictures:**

Verify the quality of the images you use in Canva designs (at least 300 PPI). Doing anything else will make things hazy. To acquire quality photos, you don't need to hire a professional photographer. Alternatively, there are photographic websites where you may get images without paying for the use rights.

🔸 **Before downloading your designs, check them:** Before you save your photos, make sure they are ready for use one final time. Is your topic too little or too large? Do your photos have a lot of clarity? Are some of your components a touch off-kilter? Consider these things. In addition to reviewing your strategy, be sure to choose the appropriate file format. You may now download your creation if everything seems to be in order.

Important Takeaways

🔸 To prevent blurry images, choose Canva's appropriate area size. Always double-check the sizing to ensure they fit, and avoid selecting lesser sizes.
🔸 Save your photos as PNG files to maintain their sharpness. This is particularly crucial if they include text.
🔸 If your drawings don't function as PNGs, save them first as PDFs and then convert them. If you want high-quality printouts, choose PDF Print.

After a lot of effort, a Canva creation might sometimes seem hazy. Don't worry, this won't occur if you use high-quality images, save your drawings as PNGs or PDFs, and utilize the appropriate paper size. To enhance your Canva project and correct any hazy designs you may have created, adhere to these suggestions.

Activities

1. What are the process of using Transparency and Gradients?
2. What do you understand by Color Theory?
3. Explain Primary, Secondary, and Tertiary color
4. Explain how to Use and Adjust Colors in Designs
5. Explain how to Prevent Canva Designs from Being Blurry

CHAPTER EIGHT
PROFESSIONAL CANVA TECHNIQUES
Features of Animation and Video

More people will notice and follow you on social media and in your marketing materials if you utilize music and video. Videos and posts that circulate on social media platforms like Facebook are popular. This is due to the fact that motion is easier for humans to comprehend than stationary images. Having the ability to create moving visuals can benefit your company.

Making presentations

The more features Canva add, the better it becomes at creating presentations. These days, you may play games and create visually appealing presentations for business or pleasure. These are excellent for training, classes, Zoom calls, or just presenting information in an entertaining manner. Canva offers a variety of layout options, but we'll continue with Presentations (16:9). **Clicking this option will bring up a new show template:**

You may have noticed that rather than running underneath one another, the video pages run down the bottom of the screen. **You can see how the pages will join together like this:**

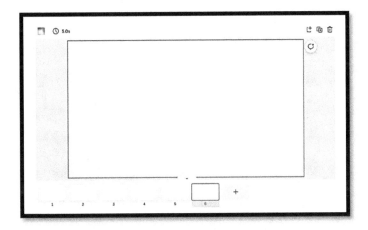

You may use shapes, photos, and other components to create your own presentation or you can choose from the various templates on the left and modify it to suit your requirements. To choose one that matches your specialty, utilize the search box at the top. Many of the templates contain many pages, as you can see when you click on them. Either click "Apply all x pages" or choose which pages to include. You may remove them one at a time if you decide to change your mind after the fact:

To demonstrate this, I've shown every page on the screen. They are now arranged in a line at the bottom. I can alter the text, images, and colors on each page to suit my brand, just as I can with any other Canva design. If you have the PRO version, click styles on the left to choose the colors you want for your brand. Next, select "Apply to all pages" to complete the process. Your brand will be shown throughout the whole conversation:

Things are beginning to change drastically now. Once you have updated the images, provided the necessary information, and removed any unnecessary pages, you may decide how to present your work.

There are four options available on the Present tab:

- **Standard:** This mode allows you to go on to the next page when you're ready and watch the program whenever you want. And there is a lot of stuff on the screen.
- **Autoplay:** You control the duration of each page's playback. After that, it will navigate through your program on its own. Additionally, PC mode is selected.
- **Presenter view:** There are two movable doors in the presenter view. The first window may be moved to the desired location on the screen that you will be seeing.

You may provide information to your audience with the second one. You may see the pages and helpful remarks for your show:

- **Present and record:** This is my preferred option as it allows you to record your speech while you deliver it. It contains a little recording of you in the corner, so it works well for classes that have previously been recorded. It will lead you to the recording room after you pick it up.

Here's where you can check if the microphone and camera are ready to record. If you choose this option, your short film will only appear in the corner of the full-screen view, while the notes will be on the right and the pages will run down the bottom. Once you've finished recording, you may save the show to your computer for later viewing or share a link to it. The computer shortcuts in presentations are something else I like. Typing tools that add tiny images around the page are now available on Canva. Look at this: **Hold down one of these keys while you speak:**

- *C*: Confetti
- *D*: Drum roll
- *Q*: Quiet emoji
- *U*: Curtains fall
- *O*: Bubbles
- *B*: Blur
- *M*: Mic drop

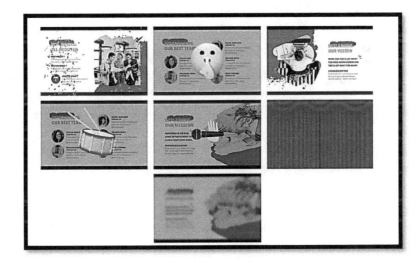

Presentations become much more entertaining with the addition of visuals. Let's now examine how to update your social media visuals and include music and video, which ought to increase your visibility.

How to Include and Modify Audio

Many people include music into their designs for video websites such as YouTube, Instagram, TikTok, and others. However, there are instances when you may not wish to listen to the movie's soundtrack. You may have also produced a silent film. Finally, to make it more engaging for viewers, you might use music. The Audio and Video choices are located on the left side of the screen after your picture is open in Canva. The Apps tab is located in the far left corner as you scroll to the bottom:

I'll go over how sound works, where to locate various sound files, and how to incorporate them into your Canva design.

- When you click on Apps, videos and audio will appear at the top of the list. If you click on each one separately, they will appear in your menu.
- To see the search results, click on Audio. In this section, we'll discuss how to include sound into your design.
  - ➢ You may locate various music genres using the options underneath the search box. However, you may scroll down to see additional popular or recently used audio files.
- Next, a play button will show up when you move your cursor over the image symbol. The sound file will play as a result. Before adding the sound to your work, click here to hear it.
- You may include a sound you like into the design when you've found it. When a portion of the sound is played, it will appear at the top. Drag the blue bar along the sound to adjust this.

- The recorded portion that will play in this instance is only five seconds long. You must alter the design's time period rather than the music file in order to alter the size. Every time, the sound will play for a certain period of time. To eliminate the sound and lengthen the design, click the trash can symbol in the upper right corner:

+ The top bar will remain the same. To alter the length of the image, enter a different time in this box and hit Enter. It always lasts five seconds.

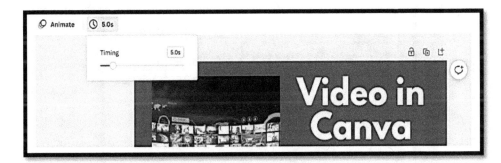

+ It will sound fantastic when you add your sound once more:

A single sound file may be added at a time. Simply add another one if you'd want to. The previous one will be replaced by it. Additionally, you may adjust the sound's volume by clicking the speaker button in the upper right corner. Next, we'll see how to add and modify a video.

How to Include and Modify Videos

There are many excellent courses on Canva. The likelihood of finding what you need is high. Additionally, you may remove the backdrops, alter them, and add videos. I should clarify, however, that this is a PRO tool. To add a video to a Canva template, use the Upload option on the left after selecting a new or existing template. Pictures and videos may now be sent from your computer. A movie will be uploaded to your template if you click on it in the upload section after adding it. You may modify it from here using the options in the top bar: When you choose the Edit video tab, this application will appear on the left side of the screen. On the right, you may adjust the brightness, contrast, color, and shade of your video.

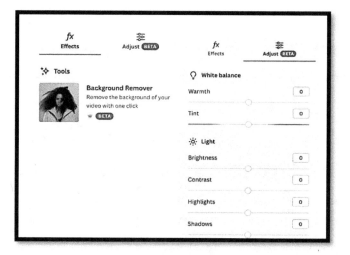

Before and after using the Background Remover software, watch this video. The ancient film with the entire backdrop is this one:

When the backdrop is removed, it looks like this:

I can now include this into any design, regardless of the color of the frame, grid, or backdrop. This will improve the appearance of my film and design. In addition, I may remove other items and add a photo to squares and frames. I can now chop and trim videos. The most of the time, I want to remove the last element that gives it an incomplete appearance, such as when I reach over to press "End" after recording. I can do this by selecting the purple lines on the top bar that indicate the start and finish of the movie, and then selecting "Done." This will make your video shorter, and you can see the change in the box on the left. Right now, it reads 9.1 seconds:

Additionally, you have two playback options. One allows you to loop the film indefinitely, meaning it will continue to play until you stop it. You may avoid pressing play each time you wish to view the movie by setting it to play automatically:

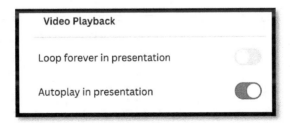

By making these white regions on top of the screen closer together, you may also adjust the size of the movie. This allows you to eliminate background objects or people. After making one last flip or turn, animate the video just like you would any other template or element.

How to Include Animation

Instead of using film, you may utilize animation. You may convert your design into an MP4 file by adding motion to it if you don't want to shoot a movie or can't locate one on Canva that suits your needs. It will continue to include social media footage and movement. Moving various elements of your design up and down and adding motion may be done in a number of ways.

It is possible to animate the following:

- The entire design is one
- Individual text boxes
- Individual elements
- Individual images and videos

Different options will appear on the left if you choose a different area of your image. After selecting a photo, text box, or feature, click "Animate" each time. On the left, a new two-column graphics box will appear. The item you choose will be on one, and the whole page will be on the other. You may choose from:

You may move your cursor over one of the boxes to see how a motion will appear in your design. If you click on Page Animations and then move your cursor over them, the same thing will occur. However, the motion will now be applied to the whole design. While the animations for elements, images, and videos are essentially the same, there are three additional options for images and videos. Additionally, you'll notice these near the bottom, which are reserved for images and videos:

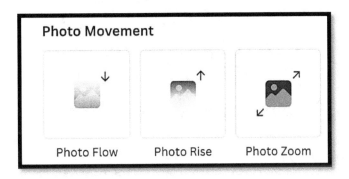

The text boxes have undergone some modifications. More options are now available to you, such the Typewriter appearance. **These may help your work stand out since they are specific to the writing:**

Using stickers and dynamic features, you may include moving elements into your design. The section on elements has the whole list. You may use this to locate movies and music as well.

Directly Recording to Canva

When you want to record anything and add it to a Canva template, this is a fantastic tool that can save you a ton of time. In other cases, adding it might need you to visit another website or snap a photo and upload it to your computer. All of this is eliminated by the record straight tool, which is also quite easy to use. You must be on the design where you want to add the recording in order to locate the feature. **I created the mock-up shown below:**

Below the text movie, I would want to add a short film to Canva. On the left side of the screen, locate the menu and choose "Uploads." **The buttons to record oneself and upload files are located here. Select:**

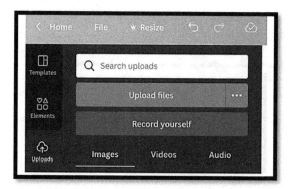

It will open a new window with a little image of you in the lower left corner and your template in the background:

Above this box are four options. They are:

- **Effects and filters:** You may alter the appearance of your movie here. There is now only one advantage, and that is the smoothing of the skin:

- **Modify the shape:** In this manner, you may choose a round or square movie.
- **A mirror camera:** This feature rotates the camera so that any text or writing is properly seen.
- **Switch off the camera:** You can only record sound with this option; the camera cannot be used. Look over this guide and don't change a thing. Simply press the record button located at the bottom. It will begin recording automatically after three, two, and one counts. Then, to indicate that you are live, a red circle with the phrase "RECORDING" within will show up. After that, click "Done." We'll process the movie for you. Then choose the "Save and exit" link located in the upper right corner. Your plan will include the video. Simply drag and drop it into the desired location. You may start using your design as soon as you save and download it. One helpful feature that saves a ton of time is the ability to record directly into Canva. You may upload your own movies or utilize the collection of movies it contains.

Making Infographics

Images that provide facts in an aesthetically pleasing and easily comprehensible manner are called infographics. You may convert complex text or numbers into easily understood images by using a user-friendly design tool such as Canva. Yes, even if you're not very good at design, you can use Canva to create charts that appear professional. You can quickly alter an infographic that has already been created or create one from scratch using Canva's drag-and-drop features.

The steps to create a chart in Canva are as follows.

- **Create an account or sign in to Canva:** Before you can create a chart, you must register or login in to Canva. To sign up, you may use your Google, Facebook, or email address.

- **Make Your Own Canvas:** After signing in, click Create a Design in the top right corner of the homepage. Search for "infographic" in the resulting search field on the next screen.

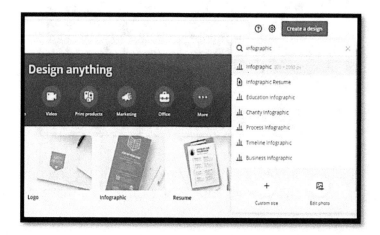

- ➢ By default, Canva will start a blank document with a 800x2000 pixel resolution when you choose "Infographic" from the search results. If you want like, you may create your own infographic from the ground up, but we'll be utilizing a pre-made design.

- **Examine Infographic Templates:** When you launch the dashboard, a number of infographic templates appear on the left side of the screen. These vary in terms of subject, color, style, and other aspects.

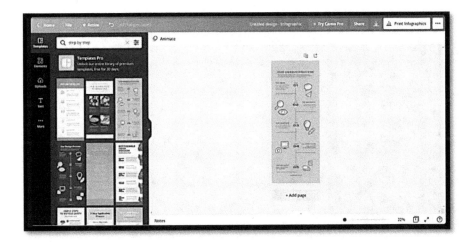

> ➤ To discover the template type you need fast, you may enter keywords into the search field. Instead, select a template that suits your message by scrolling down. To make it editable, click on it after that. You may easily include a chart to display the data as soon as you begin modifying the design.

✦ **Personalize the Background:** The backdrop included with the template may be altered to suit your requirements, or it can be kept. To change the backdrop, choose backdrop from the menu on the left. Next, choose a color or design that complements your name or personal style.

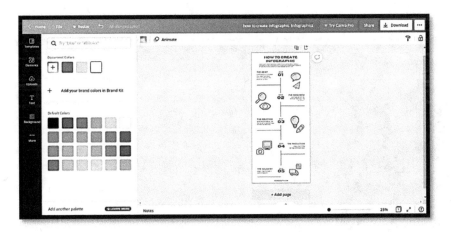

> ➤ After selecting a backdrop, you may alter its appearance using the editing menu located just above the page. Additionally, you may alter its transparency, apply effects, and change its color from the same menu.

✦ **Modify the Text:** Click on the test text to add your own content, then hit the "Delete" key to remove it. Next, type directly into the now-empty text area.

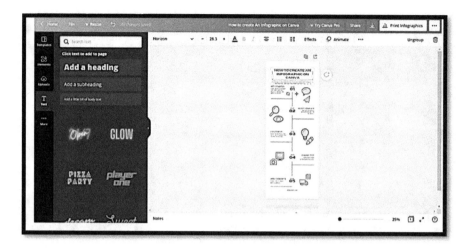

> Choose a font type, size, or color using the text toolbar at the top of the screen after selecting the word you want to alter. You can also drag and drop the fancy font you want to use on the infographic after clicking the Text option on the left side of the screen. After that, you are free to alter the size and other aspects as you see fit.

+ **Include Visual Components:** Canva organizes design components into categories such as grids, frames, charts, images, videos, lines, and shapes. Drag and drop the section you want to use into the infographic after clicking on a category.

To discover the precise image you're looking for; use the search option to refine the results. You may upload your own images or graphics to Canva and include them into the layout. Files may be moved about the template and their sizes altered. Remember that certain components are expensive to use. A crown emblem will appear in the lower right corner of everything that costs money.

How to Make Your Infographic Include a Chart

Sometimes you'll need a chart to display your data. Use these procedures to include a chart in your slideshow:

➢ Launch a template for a chart. Next, locate the "More" link on the left sidebar and choose "Charts." A variety of charts will be available for you to select from.

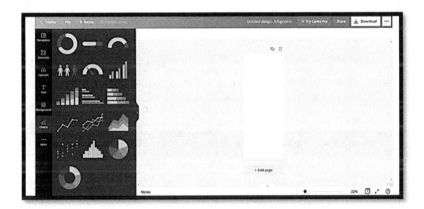

➢ Select a chart. For this, a pie chart will be used.
➢ At the top of the page is the Edit tab. To alter the picture, click it. A table including names and numbers will appear in the left sidebar.

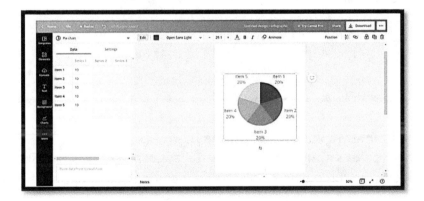

- Click on the boxes in the table to input your details. To add new rows, click on the table's bottom row.

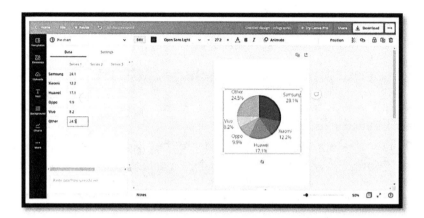

- To alter the chart's colors, choose the color tile from the menu at the top of the screen. Next, choose the color you want to use to alter the color style of the chart.

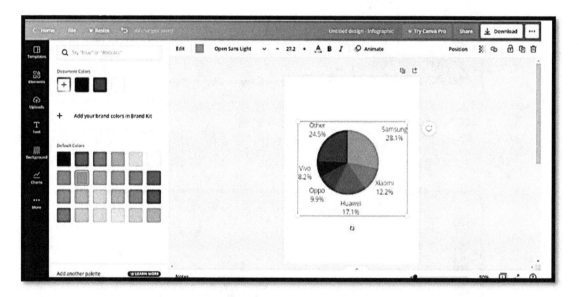

- **Save your infographic and distribute it.**
  - ➢ After you're satisfied with the chart's appearance, click the Share option by clicking the three dots in the top right corner. The infographic may be added to your website or shared directly on social media platforms.

> ➤ Click the Download icon next to Print Infographics to download it as a PNG, JPG, or PDF file.

Make Infographics for Any Need with Canva

An easy approach to display poll results or just educate someone is using an infographic. Even for those who are not artists, Canva greatly simplifies the process of creating infographics. Additionally, it allows you to create a variety of infographics, so you are not limited to a single design.

Creating Presentations

Canva is a template design website that allows you to create stunning documents, making it just as simple to create presentations as Google Slides. Below are **design guidelines for Canva presentations.**

Step One: Open Canva
> ➤ Click Presentation under Create a Design.

The search box next to "Design anything" may also be used to find "Presentation." Clicking on Presentation will lead you to a blank page. On the left is a collection of pre-made templates, just like in all of Canva's workspaces. However, it could be advisable to utilize a template if you have limited time and must create this show for work. Canva classifies these templates according to their intended usage, which ranges from pitch presentations to creative endeavors. Let's start this session by heading to the Professional Presentation section, which has templates that are ideal for our requirements. Select your favorite.

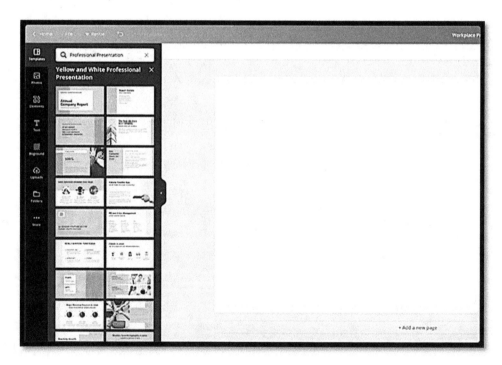

A number of distinct pages will appear on the right when you click on a design. These pages all employ the same colors and features; however they vary somewhat from one another.

Step two: Select a Page Layout and Modify Your Text

The fact that these pages don't have to be assembled a certain manner is one of Canva's many advantages. One or more designs may be used repeatedly, immediately after one another, or never at all. All you need to do is click on the blank workspace to bring your first page to life and add a design. Next, choose one of the pre-existing designs on the left by clicking on it. You may begin making adjustments when Canva loads it into the page. I decided to utilize a visually appealing design for this lesson's title page. I may write my own content and remove the blanks by clicking on each text box on this page. The Text editing box, shown in red here, allows you to adjust the size, color, weight, and spacing.

Step three: Modify Your Graphic Components

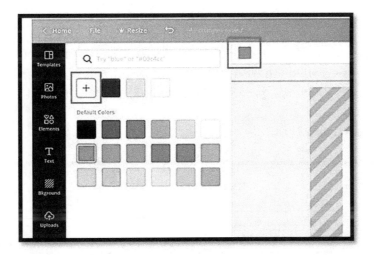

Having the appropriate amount of text—not too much—is one of the most crucial considerations while assembling your performance. Verifying that the visual components match is also crucial. With Canva, you may remove or retain as many visual elements as you choose. They may be moved about as well.

➢ Click on an element to see its bounding box in order to delete it. Click Delete.

➢ Click and drag an element around the page to move it.

At the top of the screen is the symbol for the color swatch. To alter the color of anything, click on it. You have two options: click the + symbol to open the color picker and choose your own color, or select a color sample from the pre-existing palette.

Step four: Include Notes on Pages

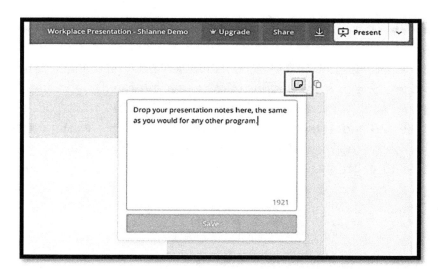

One of the last items you put to your website should be your show notes. Although it's not required, taking notes might help you recall what you want to say, particularly when you're speaking in front of an audience. Click the red "Add notes" button in the upper right corner of your Canva page. You will then see another box appear. Put your ideas in the box. You cannot, of course, exceed the word limit, but we doubt that you will. When you're finished, click Save.

Add a New Page in Step Five

The purpose of slideshows is to display a number of pages. Naturally, a single page would be a poster, so you'll likely want to include more. When you are finished completing the first page, click +Add a new page at the bottom of your area. Thanks to Canva, your show will have an additional page.

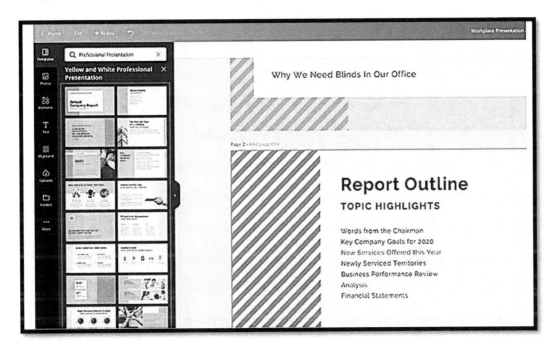

On the left side of your screen are the page designs. To alter this page's style, click on them. Click on the one you've selected.

To keep your workspace organized, you may wish to give each page a name if you're creating many pages. On your current page, look for the dotted line in the top left corner. Labels for your pages may be added here. Click on it and type something. From there, you may add a new title.

If you are completely dissatisfied with this new page, you may delete it. In the top right corner of the website is a symbol for a garbage can. Put pressure on it. Have you changed your mind, or did you accidentally hit "Delete"? You just need to click the "Undo" button located in the top left corner of your screen, so don't panic.

Step six: Include a Chart

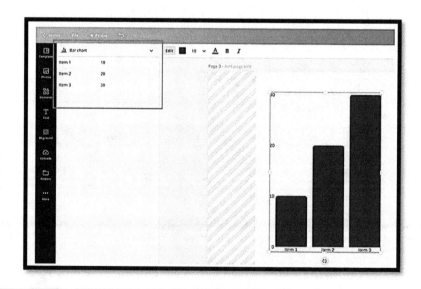

The simplicity with which you may include graphs into your presentation is one of Canva's finest features. You may then modify those graphs to suit your needs. Look for a website layout where a graph is already present. Double-clicking the graph on that page will cause its box to light up once you've added it to your presentation. The toolbar on the left will display your graph's options. The kind of graph you are using is indicated by a dropdown option at the top of those settings. A list of items and their respective values may be found underneath that. Click on each box and start typing to modify the names of these items. Click the box and enter the new amount to modify the numbers. Canva will immediately display the updated graph whenever you alter these values so you can see how it appears.

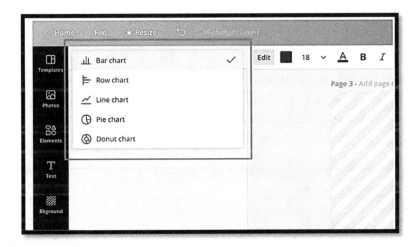

You may choose a new style by clicking on the dropdown menu whenever you wish to modify the graph's appearance. Canva will automatically alter the appearance of your graph, but the data will remain same.

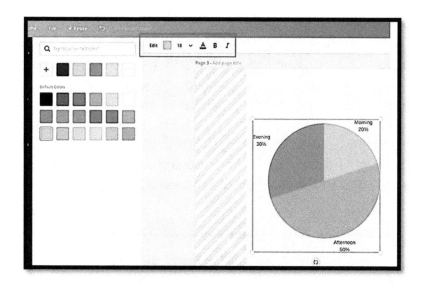

Last but not least, you may alter the graph's color. Make sure the box around your graph is chosen first. Then, in the top left corner of your screen, locate the Edit controls. To find out what works best, you should give them a try.

Step seven: Add transitions and review your presentation.

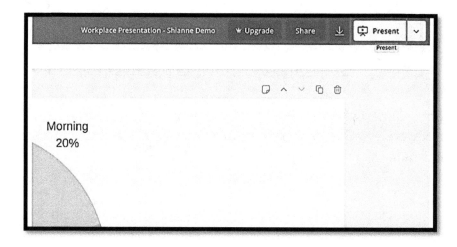

You should review your speech for errors as you wrap it up. Additionally, you may want to improve the way the pages flow together. To add seamless transitions, click the "Present" icon in the top right corner of your screen. Grab the photo.

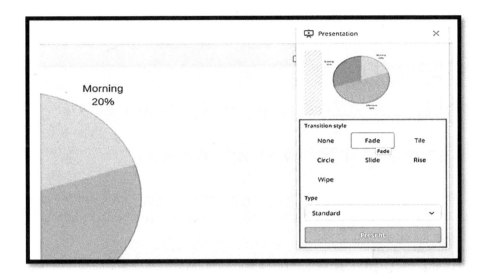

When you click on that option, Canva will provide a drop-down menu where you can choose the Transition style you want. Once you have chosen your Transition style, you may choose your Type. Once everything is adjusted, click the blue "Present" button to see your slideshow play. You can also adjust the pace at which your presentation plays using Type. It will open in full screen when you click on it, allowing you to check for errors. If you discover any errors in your presentation, you may dismiss the window by using the Escape key. After making any adjustments you believe are required, complete the design.

Step eight: Get Your Work Presentation

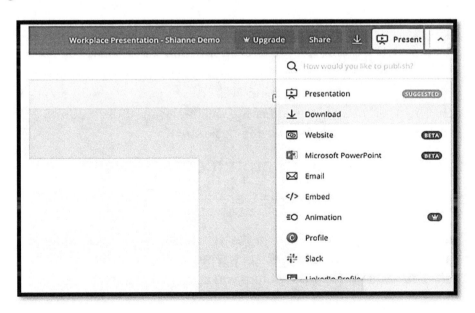

When the conversation is done, you are prepared to download. To save your presentation or use it in another way, use the dropdown menu next to the "Present" button. The majority of these options are free to use with a basic account. A gold "crown" will be placed next to those who aren't. You also have a variety of options, including posting the file on another website, emailing it to colleagues, or storing it. That's it. You're finished.

Master Your Slideshow Presentation

Now that you know how to use Canva to create a presentation for business, you can start exploring. It's preferable to experiment with the settings yourself since there are many things you can modify.

Make Your Resume with Canva

Although creating a CV is time-consuming, it is crucial, particularly if you are beginning from scratch. The good news is that there are online design tools that may assist you in creating a resume that is appropriate for the position.

Making a Resume from Scratch using Canva

How to create a resume using Canva

- **Create a New Page First:** Click on Create a Design on Canva's main page to start creating a résumé. A variety of résumé types will be returned by the search. Make sure the size is 8.5 x 11 inches before you click on Resume.

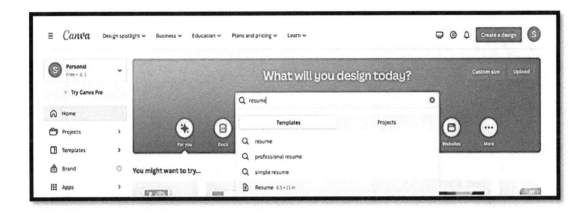

- **Modify the Background:** Blank designs start with a white page on Canva's Editor page. To alter the background's color, right-click on it and choose "Background Color." After then, you may choose a color from the selection that appears.

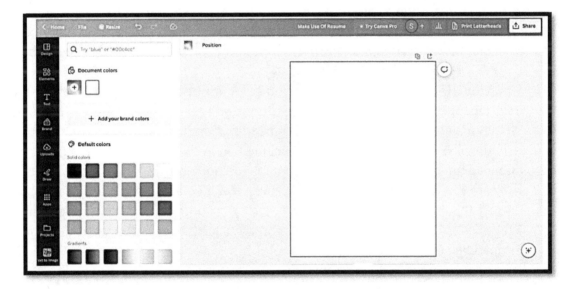

> ➤ To see even more options, you may also click the plus symbol (+) to launch the Color Picker.

- **Select Your Components:** Next, choose the Elements tab and search for the pictures and shapes. Note that components that have a crown on them are expensive since they are part of the Canva Pro subscription. It's usually a good idea to highlight your resume with a basic form. One will be selected to be used in the top right section of ours. To locate these shapes, choose Elements > Shapes > See All. Select a format that you believe will add distinction to your resume.

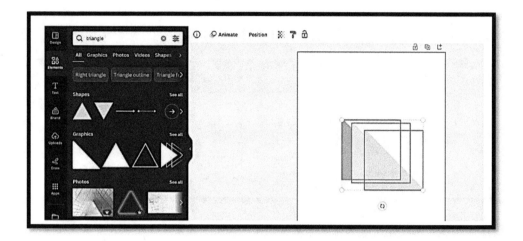

➤ If you are unable to discover a form that you like, you can always put its name into the search field. The form will appear in Shapes, Graphics, Photos, and other areas. Make care to adjust the size if necessary. Something overly large that dominates the design is not what you want. To alter the color, utilize the color picker located in the top left corner of your workspace. You can see how the form is assembled in the next step.

✦ **Put Your Header Here:** Then, after you have finished adding Items, choose the Text tab. There are several approaches to include text on your resume. You may create a variety of documents with headings and subheadings with Canva. Additionally, you have the option to include text in the body alone, a header, or a subheading. If you click on a heading/subheading combination, you can see that they are too large for the header. Moreover, it will be at the incorrect location. To correct this, shift the text box inward by clicking on one of its reference points. Move the text box to the desired location by placing your cursor over it, clicking, and holding.

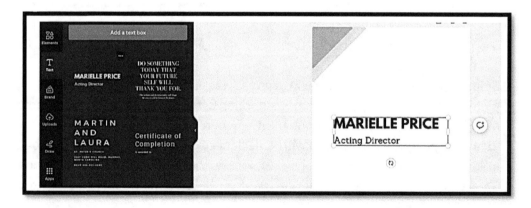

Moving the text box may cause pink lines to appear in various locations. The shapes on the page should correspond with your writing. Hints are these pink lines. Click on the Alignment button to shift your text's alignment from center to left-justified. This will display a menu with every option available to you.

To alter the style, just click on the text instead of highlighting it. Next, choose the font drop-down menu located in the top left section. From the available fonts, choose one. To alter the content, click within the box and begin typing.

⚓ Include a Professional Profile

You should have a company profile if you want to make your resume better. It should take no more than one or two sentences. This is your opportunity to demonstrate your excellence and your suitability for the position. To create your own subheading, choose create a Subheading from the Text tab. Modify the title to "Professional Profile" or any appropriate term for your company. The text box ought to appear underneath the header on the page. Select a distinct style and put it there.

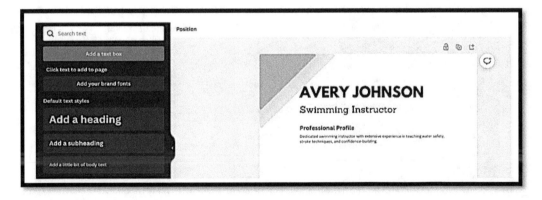

Click Add a small amount of body text after that. After selecting this, a new text box will appear where you may enter your bio. When you're finished, place it under the "Professional Profile."

✦ Include a Divider

To make your professional description stand out from the rest of your resume, you may include a visual at the conclusion. In Elements > forms > Lines, choose a line from the list of forms and lines. It shouldn't take attention away from the top of the page, provided it's simple and unobtrusive. As necessary, adjust its size and color by moving it around.

✦ Complete Your Sections

The various sections of your resume must then be completed. Provide your personal details, accomplishments, employment history, and lessons learnt. Don't include anything unnecessary in your CV. Use the same procedure you used to create the text in the previous step to add the text boxes.

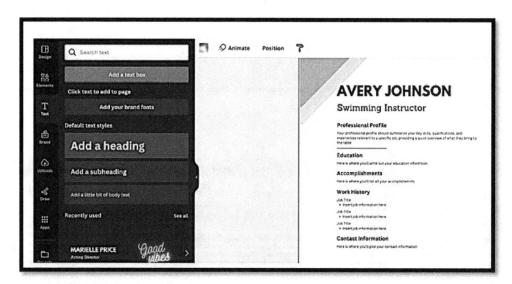

A simple method to ensure that all of your sections have the same layout is to copy the body text and subheading from the professional profile. Simply copy the text, then edit the content within the box.

⤋ Add Visual Interest or Links

To make your resume easy to read, keep it basic most of the time. However, in certain cases, using images on your online resume might improve its appearance. If you lack any relevant images, it might be quite beneficial to provide a few pertinent links, such as to your portfolio, earlier articles, personal website, etc.

Adding a link to your CV in Canva is simple. It will be connected when you've entered the desired information in the "Links" section and clicked on the words you want the link to go to. A three-dot icon will also appear if you choose the text field. After selecting Link from the three dots, enter the URL and hit Enter.

⤋ Update Your Resume and Sort the Components

Always make sure there are no grammatical or spelling errors. You may ensure that your resume seems professional by learning how to proofread it. "Grouping" indicates that various sections of your page will be seen together. These terms indicate that although you may modify each component independently in Canva, you can also move the components across the page as a unified unit. This is useful if you want to alter the design while maintaining the various components' sequence.

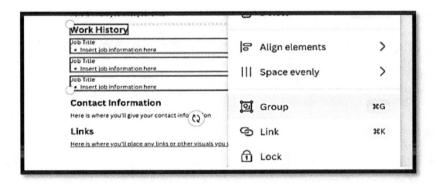

The process of grouping items involves clicking and dragging them till purple lines surround them. Once everyone has been selected, click Group. After making any last adjustments to the appearance of your resume, you're done.

Using a Template to Create a Resume on Canva

People sometimes lack the time or motivation to create a polished résumé from the ground up. **If it describes you, you should create a CV using one of Canva's templates.**

⅍ Choose a Template

Compared to creating a resume from scratch, using a template makes the process much simpler. On the Canva homepage, type "Resume" into the search field and hit "Enter." Thousands of resume templates—some even include a cover letter template—will appear on the following page. Click Customize This Template after selecting the one you believe would work best for you.

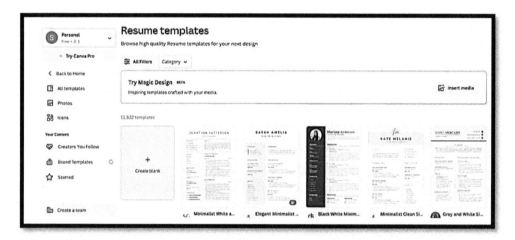

⅍ Enter your information in the template.

There are many sections in every template that you must complete. Similar to creating a resume from scratch, you may make adjustments as you go by clicking on the text box.

If you determine that some sections of the resume don't suit the format you desire, you may change or remove them. Keep in mind that you are free to alter any of the templates as you see fit.

Moving a whole section, even if just to a new page, is simpler when it is already categorized. Refer to step nine above to find out how to group a component.

Activities

1. What are the steps to create a chart in Canva?
2. What are the design guidelines for Canva Presentations?
3. Explain how to create a resume using Canva
4. Use a Template to Create a Resume on Canva

CHAPTER NINE
UTILIZING CANVA FOR BUSINESS

Making Logos

First step: log in and look for a template

To locate Canva's extensive collection of pre-made logo templates, use the search bar on the site or choose "logo" from the "You might want to try..." options after entering into your account.

This displays the vast collection of Canva templates. Although you may browse through it and see each design, you may want to utilize the filters to save time, since there are over 50,000 of them. Based on your preferred theme, style, subject, or features, you may use these options to focus your search.

As an example, consider starting a bakery. If so, you may see just the over 1,000 logos that match the "bakery" topic by using the filters. After that, you may further refine it by selecting a style, such as contemporary or simple, until you discover a logo design that you like.

If you wanted your new computer repair firm to seem strong and contemporary, you could also choose "computer" as your topic and "modern" as your style. We would like to inform you that template with a little crown symbol are only usable with Canva Pro. If you're still unsure if the platform is perfect for you, you can obtain all of the Pro-only templates and files for free for 30 days, even though it does cost $12 per month. To discover the ideal template for the kind of logo you want to create, utilize the filters. To open it in the Canva design tool, click on it.

Second Step: Select Design and Graphic Components

For this class, we decided to act as if we were launching a new travel agency and needed a logo. After launching the Canva editor and selecting our preferred logo, we must first add any photos or other elements we want to utilize.

To accomplish this, select the unwanted photographs and then hit the trash can symbol to remove them.

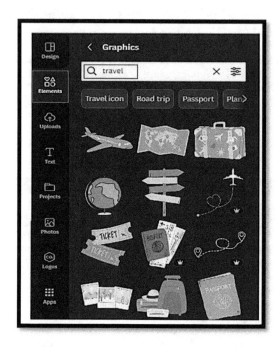

Next, choose Elements > Drawings from the Canva menu. Then, locate the drawings that are appropriate for your company by using the search feature. Here, "travel" was what we sought.

+ A picture will be added to your logo if you click on it.
+ **You may then alter it in a variety of ways, including:**
  ➢ To change its size, use the four dots in the corner.

> ➢ Changing the order of various items using the position function
> ➢ Drag the element around your design with your cursor to position it where you want it.

Continue doing this until you're prepared to go on to the next phase. As many pictures, lines, forms, or other components as you want may be added.

Third Step: Select Your Fonts and Colours

If you enjoy the way your picture appears but don't believe it matches with your brand, you can always modify the colors. Click on your photos, borders, or other elements to change their color. This will display your editing menu's color boxes in the top right corner. As you can see, these boxes are the same color as your component.

You can see the color options by tapping those boxes. Astutely, Canva will provide a list of colors that were previously used in your design.

Additionally, a list of pre-set colors is available for selection. Use the sliders, enter the hex code, or click the + symbol with the rainbow border to obtain the precise color you desire.

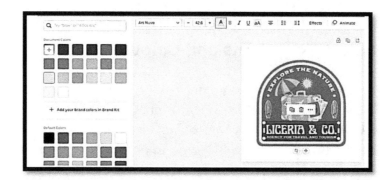

- Select the text and click the "A" symbol with a line across it to change its color.
- The color selections will be the same as in the image above.

Click on the word you want to alter the font for. This will display a menu where you may choose from a variety of typefaces.

Additionally, you can add some lovely font selections that are already assembled with your design by selecting them from the text menu.

Fourth Step: Include Your Text

- The last step is to substitute your company name for the standard text.
- That's really easy to accomplish.
- To include your small business's name, just choose the wording and underline it. Next, enter it as you would in Microsoft Office®.

Step 5: Get Your New Logo Here

Once you have completed all of that, you may make any last adjustments to your design until you are satisfied with the final logo.

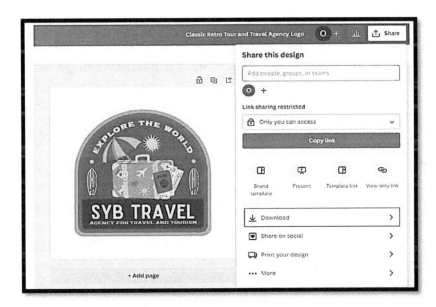

You should then get and use that picture. You may do that by selecting "Share" and then "Download." A list of file formats that you may use to save the file will appear as a result.

Creating Graphics for Social Media

- **Select the Appropriate Sizes for Every Platform:** Every social networking platform requires images to be a certain size. Selecting the ideal size from Canva's built-in options is simple, ensuring that your designs appear fantastic across all platforms.

Pro Tip: The first step is to click on Create a Design and choose from alternatives such as LinkedIn Banner (1584 x 396 px), Facebook Cover (820 x 312 px), or Instagram Post (1080 x 1080 px).

- **Begin by customizing a template:** Canva offers a vast array of templates that are specifically made for different social media platforms. Nevertheless, templates are excellent starting points, but you should modify them to distinguish your brand.

Pro Tip: Pick a template that reflects your brand's tone and style then change the fonts, colors, and photos to fit your identity.

- **Use the Fonts and Colors of Your Brand:** Repetitively using the same typefaces and colors contributes to the personality development of a brand. To make your brand's color scheme, typefaces, and logo easily accessible, use Canva Pro's Brand Kit feature.

Pro Tip: To keep things looking neat, use the Color Picker Tool to match the precise colors of your brand and limit your choice of typefaces to no more than two or three.

- **Make Use of Alignment Tools and Grids for Balance:** Images must be properly spaced and positioned to seem professional. To ensure that everything is aligned and spaced out correctly, you can use Canva's Grids and Guides to organize your design.

Pro Tip: Use the place Tool to center or equally distribute items, then enable Rulers and Guides (located under File > View) to place components exactly.

- **Pick Excellent Pictures and Illustrations:** Canva's library has a large number of images and drawings, but it's crucial to choose high-quality ones that complement your message.

Pro Tip: To locate photos that fit your style, use keywords like "bold," "modern," or "minimal" in the Photos tab. Prior to incorporating them into your design, always verify the quality and resolution.

- **Use Text Overlays to Send Powerful Messages:** Adding text backgrounds is a fantastic technique to make your message stand out. Use strong, readable fonts for headlines, and consider using them with smaller subheadings for context.

Pro Tip: To make your text stand out, use Text Effects like Lift or Shadow. You may also play about with the Transparency settings to create a layered appearance.

- **To Improve Visual Appeal, Use Shapes and Icons:** Shapes and icons may be used to break up or highlight key information. Canva's library has a large number of shapes and icons that may be altered in terms of size, color, and arrangement.

Pro Tip: Look for visual components that direct the viewer's attention through your design by searching for "Social Media Icons" or "Arrow Shapes."

- **Use Canva's Effects and Filters to Create a Coherent Look:** Your design's whole vibe may be altered using effects and filters. You may use Canva's built-in filters to make all of your drawings seem the same.

Pro Tip: Click on your picture, choose Filters, and then try out Retro, Grayscale, or Dramatic. For modest improvements, change the intensity.

- **Develop Reusable Templates to Ensure Uniformity:** reating reusable templates can help you save time and maintain consistency if you post often on social media.

Pro Tip: Create a few basic templates for various post kinds (such as announcements, promotions, and quotations) and save them in your Canva folder. Simply change the photos and text as necessary.

- **Use the Correct Format for Exporting:** Make sure your images are exported in the optimal format for social media so they seem crisp and expert:
  - **PNG:** Ideal for pictures with clear backgrounds or excellent graphics.
  - **JPEG:** Perfect for pictures and gradients.
  - **MP4:** For animated postings or little video snippets.

Pro Tip: To guarantee quick loading speeds on social networking sites, always verify the file size and resolution.

Activities

1. **In utilizing Canva for business, explain how to:**
- Make Logos
- Create Graphics for Social Media

CHAPTER TEN

CUSTOMIZATION AND CANVA TEMPLATES

Changing Templates That Have Been Pre-Designed

Choosing the Appropriate Template

The first step in altering a pre-made design is to choose a template that meets your requirements. You may use keywords like "Instagram post," "holiday sale," or "motivational quotes" to locate templates while creating an Instagram post, for example. Additionally, Canva allows you to arrange templates according to certain groups, topics, or dimensions. You save time by not having to start from scratch thanks to this feature. After selecting a template, you may open it directly in the Canva editor. This is where customization is most effective.

Changing the Text

One of the simplest and most practical methods to modify a template is to alter the text. You may alter the example text in the Canva templates to see how the style will appear with actual text. All you have to do is click on the text boxes and fill them in with your own thoughts. You may include quotations, company names, event information, and anything else that complements your design. In addition to modifying the text, you may alter its font, size, color, alignment, and spacing in Canva. Canva has a vast font collection that includes anything from bold display fonts to elegant designs. If you're working on a brand project, you may utilize typefaces that complement your brand or share your own fonts. Simply drag and resize the text boxes to better suit the layout in order to update the wording. You may also use background colors, outlines, or shadows to make the text stand out.

Variations in Color

Colors have a big role in how well your design looks. Canva makes it simple to alter the colors of text, backgrounds, and other design elements. If you are dealing with a brand theme, you may utilize particular hex codes to maintain consistency. To discover colors that complement one another, you may also experiment with the color wheel. There are other color tones to pick from. With Canva, you can add textured backgrounds, transparency effects, and gradients, giving you a lot of creative flexibility. If you're not happy with the color scheme of the template you've selected, you may alter it entirely by selecting "Change All." This instantly updates the template to use the new color scheme you selected.

Image Editing

You may use the images or sketches included in templates as placeholders to demonstrate how your design could appear. You may alter these images to your own or browse Canva's extensive library of both free and premium stock images. You can upload your own photographs in two simple ways: either click the "Upload" button or drag & drop them into the Canva editor. Once you've placed the photos, you may modify them to match the placeholders on the template. Canva's editing tools allow you to move, crop, and resize images. You may also alter the brightness, contrast, and saturation, apply overlays, and apply filters for a more distinctive look. You may alter and add a distinctive style to your photos using Canva's effects, such as pixelation and duotones.

Layout Rearranging

You are not restricted to the style that comes with Canva templates since you may alter them as you want. If you wish to highlight a certain area of the design or feel that other areas are too crowded, you may alter the components as necessary. Text boxes, photos, and icons may all be resized, rotated, or moved using a simple drag-and-drop operation. You may use Canva without any issues if you like to add extra pieces. For instance, you may add extra text, icons, or ornamental shapes to enhance the design. However, if you feel that a template has too many components, you may simplify the design by removing those that you don't need.

Making Use of Canva's Integrated Features

Additionally, Canva offers more sophisticated tools that you may utilize to further refine your edits. For instance:

- **Grid and Snap Features:** These tools assist you in properly aligning pieces, creating a neat and polished layout.
- **Layering:** You may move items forward or backward in Canva to alter their arrangement. Your design gains depth as a result.
- **Group and Ungroup:** This function enables you to modify many items simultaneously or divide them apart for more individualized adjustments.

Including Visuals and Icons

Canva's collection has hundreds of both free and premium icons and visuals that you can use in your design. To make these photos match your design precisely, you may search for them and alter their size, color, and positioning. For instance, you can add a phone or a location tag to a company flier to make it more functional.

Completing Your Design

Canva offers you many options for completing your design if you're satisfied with the modifications you've made. A variety of file formats, including PNG, JPG, and PDF, are available for download. You have the option to save your animation or film as an MP4. Sharing your design on social media or sending it to someone via email doesn't need you to exit Canva; you can do it directly within the app.

Make a Canva template and publish it

If you know how to utilize Canva to create designs, creating your own templates will be simple. **It simply takes a couple more steps from design to template creation.**
First Step: Sign up for Canva Pro
To create reusable designs or templates, you must have a Canva Pro account. Only Canva Pro users are able to save it as a template, but you may create one just like any other Canva design process. You must log in after creating your Canva Pro account.
Second Step: Make a layout
Click on Create a Design in the upper right corner of Canva's homepage. You may choose one of the popular social media sizes from the little dropdown box. You may also choose Custom Size at the bottom and enter your own measurements if you are certain of the project's precise dimensions.

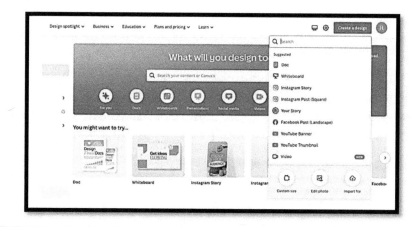

You may also enter the kind of media you want to design for in the menu's search field. Next, choose the outcome from the shown list.

Third Step: Create a Template

You may create your design as you like with Canva's editor. Include text, images, and a backdrop. Configure it how you would want your template design to appear. Consider how the design may alter if additional pictures or word lengths become available in the future when creating a template that may be used for a variety of purposes.

Fourth Step: Make Your Canva Template Public

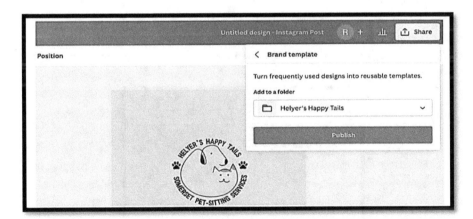

Once your design is complete, choose Share > Brand Template. You may choose a folder to save your template here. To save the template in the folder, click Publish or Add. A link that allows others to see your template design is created when you save or publish it. Copy and paste the link to share.

Fifth Step: Access and Modify the Template You Saved

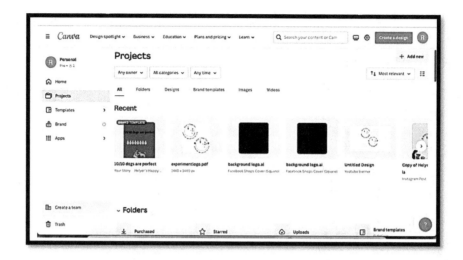

Saving your template is essential for future usage. To access it, click the menu on the left side of the Canva homepage. Your most recent projects are shown on the Projects page. You can see where you stored your templates underneath them. To open a template in the editing window, locate it and click on it. Like any other Canva project, you may make the necessary changes to the template and then save it. After then, you are free to utilize it as you see fit.

How to Use a Phone or Tablet to Create and Share a Canva Template

The majority of the Canva features are available on your PC and mobile device. You can create Canva templates on your phone or tablet in a few easy steps.

164

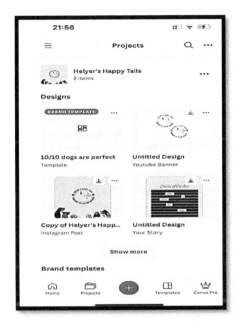

- Log into your account on Canva Pro.
- To begin a new design, press +.
- Create your own layout.
- Select a folder by going to Share > Brand Template.
- To access your stored templates, tap Projects.

Is It Possible to Import a Premade Canva Template?

AI, PSD, and PDF files created elsewhere can be imported. However, when you import PSD or AI files into Canva, you are unable to modify individual components, so these cannot be used with editable Canva templates. The good news is that you can alter PDFs using Canva. You can use your designs created in Photoshop, Illustrator, or InDesign as templates by saving them as PDFs. To create templates in Canva rather than PSDs or other unchangeable formats, you can import individual components that you've created elsewhere. You can add all of your own design elements when using Canva's template-making feature. When you use Canva's provided elements, other users' template designs will differ from yours.

Make Workflow Easier with Canva Templates

Canva makes a living by using pre-made template designs for various purposes. Using Canva allows you to start from scratch, but creating your own template simplifies the process when you need to create numerous identical designs. By creating templates with Canva Pro, you can save time later. If someone purchases your designs and decides not to create their own, you may even profit.

Activities

1. Explain how to choose appropriate templates
2. Make Use of Canva's Integrated Features
3. Explain the steps for making a Canva template and publishing it
4. Explain how to Use a Phone or Tablet to Create and Share a Canva Template
5. Is It Possible to Import a Premade Canva Template?

CHAPTER ELEVEN
ABOUT CANVA PRO AND CANVA APP

How to Use the Canva App

The Home, Projects, Templates, and Canva Pro panels comprise the major section of the program. Let's review each section and its contents.

The Home Screen

The first item you see when you log in and launch the app is called "Home," so let's start there. It's quite easy to use since it appears like other social applications. The menu button is located at the top of the screen. It allows you to open Projects and Templates, among other things, much like the tabs. You can only access Brand Hub and Content Planner as a Pro member. But you can also link more sophisticated programs and applications, like Smartmokups, to Canva. Beside the options is a search bar. You may use keywords to locate templates or projects that you have already completed. You may see the thousands of templates that are included with the program by clicking on the tabs below that. Depending on how you use Canva, "For You" will change every time you use the app, just as Spotify does. It will often display your most recent work along with various design sizes and templates that you may find useful. Each one will have a conspicuous label indicating its purpose. In other tabs, you may begin working on other templates, such as those for presentations, social media, movies, prints, and more. If you click on any of them, the website will alter to show you all the things you can do about that topic.

There are many methods to begin creating a fresh image from the home screen. Clicking on a template you like will open a new window where you can start editing it. To create a design, choose the desired design type, such as mobile video or Instagram post. This page gives you the option to start from scratch or choose a template. Additionally, to restart, click the purple plus (+) symbol at the bottom of the screen. When you press it, you may choose the size (Custom or something like Facebook Post). A fresh, vacant spot will then show up.

The Screen for Projects

On the Projects page, you can see everything you've created on your computer, phone, or account. Your cloud-stored data, images, and ideas are visible to you. Each sketching image has two buttons in the top right corner. The three dots symbol opens a menu with several choices, including Edit; Make a Copy, and Share, while the arrow icon allows you to download the image.

Keep in mind that Edit will alter your previous image. If you enjoy your design and would want to save it for later use, click "Make a Copy" instead.

The Screen of Templates

This one is more about templates; however it's similar to the main screen. Using the buttons at the top, you may browse each template or by topic. You may also see the themes that other Canva users have chosen, such Juneteenth or Earth Day. Seasons or holidays are often to blame. Features Collections, Trending near You, New on Canva, and more sections are available. They're all designed to inspire you.

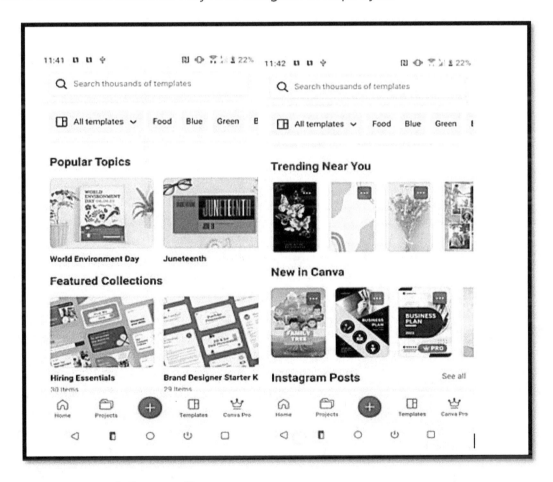

The screen of Canva Pro

If you pay for the service, you may see the final image. Options like Brand Kit, Premium Content, and social media programs are available here.

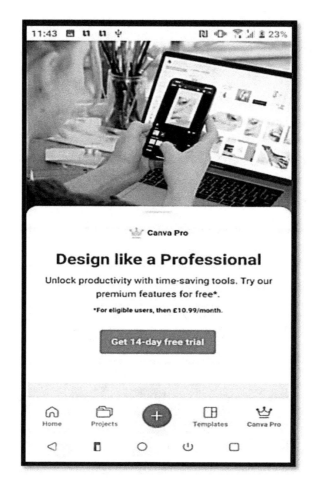

Make Your Own Design and Adjust It

Let's now discuss the tools available for creating pictures. Select a template to get started. We made advantage of an Instagram post. Note that not every template is compatible with a free account. Look for templates without the terms "Pro" or "Paid." You may alter any aspect of this image by clicking on the text, images, background, or shapes. Additionally, you may move it about, and the software will assist you with aligning objects in the center of the photo or with other objects. The controls for Undo and Redo are located in the top left corner. They resemble a pair of circular lines pointing in opposite directions. Click on any of the modifications you made that you dislike. A new set of options appears when you touch on a different area of the screen. The bar at the bottom of the screen contains them. This image has a "Replace" button on it. Pressing it allows you to choose a photo from Canva, snap a picture with your camera, or upload one from your phone's gallery.

Additionally, you may trim the image, apply effects and colors, make it move, and more. Press Edit after you've tapped a text area once to make changes. After that, you may alter the layout, size, style, and other elements. The Nudge tool has a significant impact. The distance between each direction button push is one pixel. Compared to a touch screen, this operates more precisely. Additionally, you can use the addition (+) button to add new elements to the design. From that page, you may access all of your files, add music and images, change the background, and modify the template (which will replace the existing template).

Share or Download Your Canva Design

Now is the moment to utilize the image (or film) that you have meticulously altered to perfection. Press the buttons at the top of the screen to do that. The up button allows you to share the image with others, while the down arrow stores it to your phone. One of the best features of the Canva app is the Share button. You may email your finished photo directly to friends or coworkers via Slack or WhatsApp. You may also upload your photo directly to Instagram or TikTok by clicking the "Share" button. You would need to transfer the image to your phone first if you were on a computer. If you have a Pro account, you can even schedule the post to appear on social media at a certain time.

The distinctions between desktop and mobile

Because of its multifunctional design, users may utilize the Canva app on both desktop and mobile platforms. Both have the same fundamental functionality; however they vary greatly in terms of features, usability, and interface. Understanding these variations might assist you in selecting the ideal solution for your requirements or in determining how to enhance your productivity while alternating between devices.

Version for Desktop

On a laptop, you may access Canva via a desktop application or a web browser. This version is ideal for designs with a lot of minor details since it has a larger surface and more sophisticated tools. Because the screen is larger, you can view your project more clearly and work on intricate ideas or multitask. The desktop version's toolbar and sidebar, which neatly arrange all the functionality, make it simple to use. This facilitates access to tools such as text editing, picture editing, and layer addition. Items are easy to drag and drop, and utilizing a mouse or keyboard improves accuracy, particularly when scaling, cropping, or aligning objects. Additionally, the PC version is superior for multitasking. Users may start and move between tabs or projects with ease. When working on designs that must seem the same across all formats or organizing large campaigns, this is useful. Another advantage of the desktop is its compatibility with external tools. Sharing files from your computer is simple, you can use shortcuts to expedite activities, and you can even link to third-party applications to do tasks like data import or export. As long as everyone has a steady internet connection, which is often achievable on desktop PCs, Canva's robust collaboration features enable teams to work on projects together in real-time, with notes and shared access.

The Version for Mobile

You may utilize the mobile version of Canva, which is intended to be user-friendly and portable, by downloading the app for smartphones and tablets. It is designed for managing smaller, easier tasks, making changes quickly, and working while on the move. The user interface is compact and optimized for touch displays. You can add text, alter layouts, and add components with a few touches. However, the smaller screen size might be an issue when working on designs with many layers or little elements. Scrolling and zooming are more common on mobile devices, and some users could find it more difficult to maintain accuracy without a mouse or keyboard. The mobile app is limited in its capabilities compared to Canva. Advanced features like motion effects, background removal, and multi-page browsing may not function as well or be as user-friendly as they are on the desktop. Uploading files may be a bit of a hassle on mobile devices since they might not have as much storage capacity or as much processing power as desktop computers, particularly for larger projects. On the other hand, the mobile app is fantastic as it enables you to download or share designs instantly to chat applications, email, and social networking websites. For social media administrators or consumers who want immediate results, this makes it an excellent option.

Performance

Generally speaking, desktop computers process information more quickly, particularly when working on projects that include several layers, high-resolution images, or animation effects. In contrast, mobile devices rely heavily on the speed of the internet and the capabilities of the device. People who need to work remotely but don't want to carry around a smartphone might benefit from tablets. Although they are lightweight and compact, their displays are larger than those of smartphones.

Features of Canva Pro

An overview of Canva Pro

To use Canva Pro, you may either subscribe once a month or once a year. Canva's latest version is superior to the previous one. It contains many features and capabilities designed to satisfy the needs of professional designers. Canva Pro users get access to a vast collection of templates that can be used for a variety of projects, including posters, slideshows, social media posts, and more. To enhance the appearance of their projects, customers may also access a vast collection of excellent images, movies, and musical compositions. Canva Pro is fantastic since it offers a plethora of options to assist you complete your task. Among them is Magic Resize. Without having to start from scratch, it enables users to swiftly modify designs to match various sizes. By centralizing all of their logos, colors, and fonts, users can create and maintain the visual identity of their company using the company Kit application. Users may edit files and share them instantly using Canva Pro. Because of this, it's ideal for collaborative undertakings. Users may easily arrange their drawings using folders, and they have limitless space thanks to Canva's online storage.

Canva Pro-only features

- **Magic Resize:** This feature makes it simple for users to resize designs to accommodate various screen sizes. Because layouts don't need to be modified for every device, it saves time and effort.

173

- **Brand Kit:** By using their own typefaces, colors, and logos, users can clearly define the style of their brand in all creations. This tool ensures that visual branding is done consistently and professionally.
- **Background Remover:** This tool makes picture editing simpler by removing backgrounds with a single click. This function allows you to create layouts that seem neat and expert.
- **Premium Templates:** A vast collection of beautifully designed templates for a variety of tasks, including advertisements, presentations, social media photos, and more, are available to you. These templates provide you a solid foundation on which to swiftly create visually appealing material.
- **Collaboration Tools:** Canva Pro facilitates teamwork by enabling real-time file sharing and editing. Individuals may exchange ideas and provide comments on one other are work. This helps the task go quicker.
- **Animation:** By adding movement and interactivity, animations enhance the visual appeal of designs. You may create social media postings, live presentations, and other types of multimedia material using this program.
- **Unlimited Folders and Storage:** Canva's cloud storage allows you to safely save your files and arrange your drawings in an instant with an infinite number of folders. This ensures that users may access their work from any location and do their duties effectively.
- **Priority Support:** You may contact Canva's support staff more quickly. They are accessible to assist with any queries or concerns about technology twenty-four hours a day, seven days a week. This ensures that those in need of assistance get it promptly.

Making Use of Canva Pro Tools

Resize Magic

This is Canva Magic Resize, a useful tool. Instead of starting from scratch, it enables you to swiftly and simply adjust the scale of your designs for various platforms. This enables you to create a group of images that will be used and shown uniformly across all of your websites. **Here's how you do it.**
- Create an image that will promote your business from a blank canvas.
- Click the "Resize" button in the upper left corner of your screen if you're satisfied with the change.
- A drop-down option that allows you to alter the picture's size for various social networking platforms will then appear. You may also create a post in whatever size you desire using the "custom size" option.

- To alter the size of the platform or platforms, click the "Create" button next to them. Each time you adjust an item's size in Canva, a new tab will appear.
- To obtain the greatest appearance, you will need to make adjustments to each post since they won't be altered precisely. You will ensure that your company remains unchanged and save a great deal of time.
- When you're finished with your photos, you can save or share them directly from Canva.

Using Pro to create your brand kit

Your Canva profile has the brand kit. You may access the page containing the picture by clicking on the "Brand" link in the left bar. You may create a new kit or access an existing one by clicking the "Add new" button in the upper right corner of this page. **I assembled the following two brand kits:**

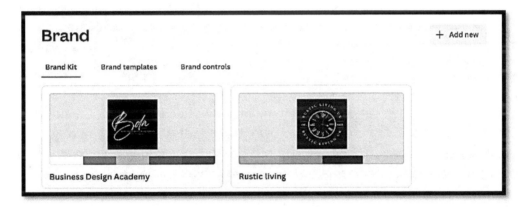

You may create a new kit by selecting "Add new" and then "Brand Kit." **You can also create brand templates here that you can use again and again, which will help you keep consistent with your brand:**

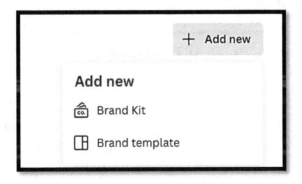

175

It's not necessary to rename your kit at this time. Then select Make. We now have an empty kit that is prepared for filling:

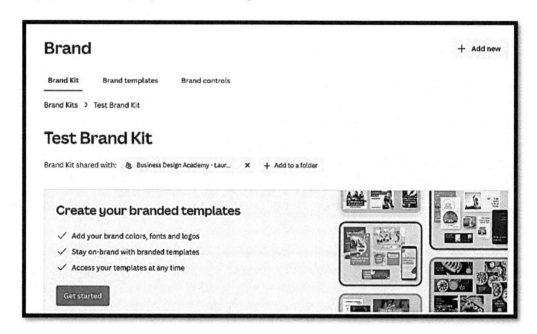

You may create your first set of named templates by selecting "Quick Create" from the "Get Started" button. If you created your own, that's fantastic, but if you're just getting started, a template is preferable. Let's add our photo by heading down to "logo." To be included, the logo has to be an image. If you haven't already, you will need to download your picture. Select Download after clicking the Share icon at the top of the picture. For you, the format will be set to PNG. Then save it to your PC or phone. We must return to the brand kit we created previously and locate it under "Brand Logos." Then, click the plus symbol to add our logo. Now, it will appear where the + symbol was. Your picture is **now included in the brand kit. You can now use the same technique to any other logos or sub-logos you own:**

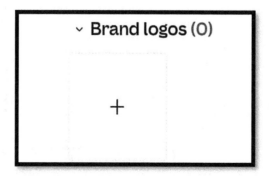

We'll now add the colors of our brand. Did you write down your HEX digits from the list of colors? You are in urgent need of them. **The color scheme I created from an image of a pink blossom will be used:**

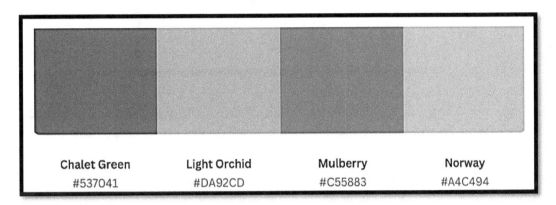

Chalet Green	Light Orchid	Mulberry	Norway
#537041	#DA92CD	#C55883	#A4C494

To create a new color pattern, click the + symbol next to the color palette. This implies that we are now free to use whatever hue we choose. To achieve the precise color your brand requires, copy and paste your HEX code or move the white circle around to modify the color. All four of my color scheme's hex numbers were copied and pasted across. To add each hue, I repeated the process and hit the + symbol. This color combination is new to me.

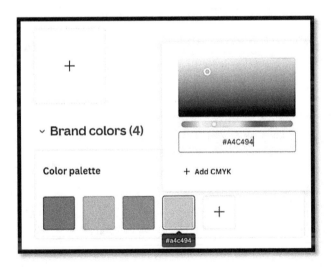

You may add as many as you want by clicking the + symbol at the top of the color pallet section. If you need to utilize various colors for different occupations, for example, you may add as many as you really need.

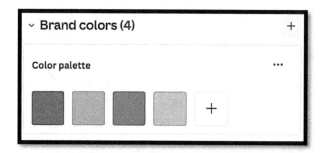

We'll look at adding our typefaces in this last section. You may add your title, subtitle, and body fonts in these three locations. You may choose your kind using the Canva drop-down menu. **Clicking on each one will allow you to:**

Add the typefaces associated with your brand to each of the three boxes in the same way. What happens if you are unable to locate the required font? **You can add these fonts to Canva if you have a Pro account:**

You must confirm that the font is the correct file type before sending it. This is often an OTF or TTF file. When you purchase or download the source font, you will get them. Once the file has been located, click "Upload a font". It will then be placed here for your use. When you are sketching, it will also appear in the font list.

Make Your Own Brand Kit with No Cost

Creating a brand kit for Pro users is as simple as that. These options are not available to free users. Adding three colors to a palette is one way to use the HEX numerals. To create your kit, you may alternatively use a Canva template. You may use the following search phrases to locate templates: "Brandboard," "Moodboard," and "Brand kit." Pick the one that appeals to you, but remember that you can alter any element of it:

Both the brand board and the moodboard have their own components, so pay particular attention to both. **Additionally, brand board label layouts will provide font selections and perhaps submark locations:**

179

I choose this template to demonstrate its appearance to you:

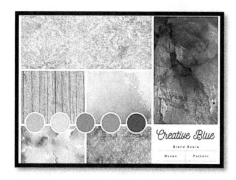

Numerous typefaces, color rings, and photo blocks are included in this design. You may either upload your own image to Canva or utilize one of the pre-existing ones and drag it into the blank area to alter any of the images. Any existing photos will be replaced by this one. When you click on a color circle, you may add your HEX numbers. **Clicking the + symbol next to the color will also allow you to add your HEX code:**

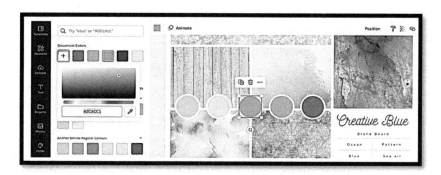

Not to mention, you may alter the look to fit your brand. To change the font, click on the text box and choose it from the drop-down menu. Numerous free typefaces are available for selection. **Altering the text to the font's name is another option:**

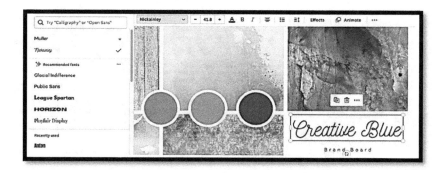

This is the most stylish approach to assemble your brand kit. Which you may print out and display. You may modify the template and reprint it as your company expands and your brand evolves. However, these left-hand alternatives will not appear while you are creating graphics for your company. Only if you have Pro and have configured the brand kit will they be on your account.

Planner for Content

Creating content for social media that people want to read is challenging and crucial. Equally crucial is making sure it launches at the ideal moment for your audience. Canva's Content Planner has made this process quite simple. In this manner, you may plan your articles for the most effective days, hours, and weeks in advance and monitor the quantity of views, clicks, likes, and comments they get. Create a strategy for your usage of social media. You will do better on it as a result.

With Just a Few Clicks, Post your Content

It's likely that you already know how to utilize Canva to create social media-worthy video and photo postings. Previously, you could download your photos and upload them to a social media platform or a planning tool for the next day. Because it allows you to plan, organize, and even publish your material directly from Canva, this new habit will save you a ton of time. You can create, distribute, and see statistics from one location when you utilize the content planner that comes with Canva.

A Simple Approach to Social Media Content Planning

You should be aware that Canva Pro includes the Content Planner. The Background Remover and the Magic Switch are available to you as a Canva Pro member. These two tools are quite popular and save people a great deal of time. To see whether you enjoy what Canva Pro has to offer, you can test it for free for 30 days.

A calendar is necessary for any plan

To access the calendar, select "Content Planner" on Canva's main page. This is a list of the things you plan to share on social media in the coming weeks. Numerous well-known cyberdates from across the globe are already included. Get suggestions for articles and methods to express yourself using hashtags that might get a lot of attention and become well-known. These will disappear if you choose "filters" and uncheck the "social media holidays" option. After this, you'll start afresh. Additionally, you might include holidays, birthdays, and local events that are significant to your company.

Plan an Already-Existing Design

It is really easy to set up timings for items. Locate a date on your calendar and click the "+" symbol in the Content Planner. You may use a template, start a new design from scratch, or see your most recent work here. Simply click on an already-made image, choose the channel, and add a description to utilize it. You may either store it as a draft to complete later or set it to happen immediately. If you so choose, you may edit or remove your post at any moment.

Setting up New Designs

Click "new" and then "post." Writing content is made simpler by the abundance of templates available. You may adjust their sizes to make them compatible with any computer by using the Magic Switch Tool (opens in a new tab or window). Yes, you may start anew by using a different image. You may customize the design anyway you wish by altering the colors and adding new text. Then it's time to start planning. After that, I only need to choose where I want to publish it by clicking "share" and then "share on social." Finally, title your post, adjust the date if necessary and either schedule it or put it on hold.

Background Remover

Up to 500 photos may have their backgrounds removed in a 24-hour period. Only images less than 9MB may currently be utilized with Background Remover. Any photo you submit that is larger than 10MP will not have a backdrop. It will be reduced in size to 10MP. The backgrounds of images you upload to "Project" files may be removed. However, the Erase and Restore brushes will not be available to you. Canva Picture Maker has additional information about it.

To eliminate a desktop computer's backdrop in the Canva Editor, just:

+ You may choose a photo from our collection or submit your own.
+ Click the "Edit Image" button on the top toolbar.
+ In the resulting left-hand panel, choose "Background Remover."
+ Next, choose "Erase" to remove the backdrop.
+ The backdrop will magically vanish once you choose "Erase."
+ Click "Apply" to save the modifications after you're satisfied with the way your photo appears without a backdrop. However, you may also choose "Restore" to undo any modifications.
+ Lastly, all you need to do is drag your updated image into position.

To eliminate a mobile backdrop in the Canva Editor, just:
- Click the image you want to modify.
- Choose "Effects" from the tool list underneath the editor.
- Press the "Background Remover." button.
- Wait the processing of the backdrop.

Using the Tool to Remove Backgrounds from Your Videos

Currently, you can only remove backgrounds from movies that are under 90 seconds long. This tool will not function if you edit a video in Canva. You would need to download and submit it once again. Additionally, sharing videos from your phone's Gallery or Camera Roll is not available. You must utilize the Uploads tab instead.

On your desktop PC, you may easily remove the backdrop from a movie by:
- Select the video that you want to edit.
- Select "Edit video" from the window that shows up above the editor.
- Press "Background Remover" in the adjacent box.
- While the background works, kindly wait.

Just follow these steps to get rid of the backdrop from a mobile video:
- Select the video that you want to edit.
- Click the "Effects" option on the menu under the writer.
- Press the "Background Remover." button.
- While the background works, kindly wait.

Editing Background Remover-Created Images with the Erase and Restore Brushes

For present, these capabilities are limited to the PC app and canva.com.
- Click on the "Erase" or "Restore" brush after selecting "Background Remover."
- Click and drag the brush over areas of the image to view or restore them.
- Using this tool, you may adjust the brush size. To adjust its size, click on it and drag it to the left or right.
- To see the initial image while you're editing, choose "Show original image."
- Using the tools at the top of the screen, choose "Done".
- At the end of your edits, click "Apply" at the bottom of the sidebar.

The Background Remover tool allows you to experiment with numerous backgrounds that either complement your brand and style or contrast with it once you know how to utilize it. Removing your buddy from a photo is not enough to remove the backdrop on social media. Ensuring that the individuals you want to see your project can view the images and designs you have created is also crucial.

Activities

1. Explain how to use Canva App
2. Discuss the Canva Pro-only features
3. Use Canva Pro to create your brand kit
4. Explain every about background remover

CHAPTER TWELVE
ABOUT DESIGN EXPORT AND SHARING

Design Downloads

- On the menu bar of the editor, choose the Share button.
- Select "Download."
- Select a file type to download from the list.
- If your design has many pages, choose the ones you want to download from the dropdown option. Next, choose "Done."
- Press the "Get" button.
- To purchase licensed versions of certain components in your design, use the "More" button next to "Try Canva for Pro/Teams for free." Click "Pay and Download" to complete the process after selecting your preferred payment method.

The download folder included with your device contains the desired image.

File Types Supported for Download

Keep your ideas in a manner that allows you to do with them what you want:

Picture

- **JPG:** Smaller picture files are more effective. To alter their size and color, slide each one.
- **PNG:** It allows you to employ transparency* and works well for photos. Move the scale to 0.5x, 1x, 2x, or 3x and check the box next to Compress file size to alter the compression ratio.
- **SVG:** Regardless of the size, the image quality remains constant. It's excellent for creating online pictures.

The quality, size, compression, CMYK color schemes, and PNG and SVG files that are shown are all modifiable by users of Canva Pro, Canva Teams, Canva for Education, and Canva for Nonprofits.

The document

- **The PDF Standard:** 96 dots per inch (dpi) or higher for graphics, text, and images

- **Printing in PDF format:** When printing at 300 dpi, you may add bleed and crop marks and choose between an RGB or CMYK color scheme.
- **Microsoft PowerPoint (PPTX):** To be used only for conversations. Other design kinds cannot currently be downloaded as PPTX.
- **Microsoft Word (DOCX):** works only with Canva Docs. Only certain design kinds are currently available for download in DOCX format.

Designs may not seem the same in Word or PowerPoint if you get them as DOCX or PPTX files. It may be necessary to make some adjustments or download the fonts you used in Canva to your phone. Movies and animations cannot currently be added to Microsoft Word and PowerPoint. You may not get the desired results from animated elements and/or movies if you save your design as a PPTX or DOCX file.

A video

- **GIF:** For designs that are animated or have moving parts
- **MP4:** Designs may include music and videos.Using Links or Emails to Share Designs

You can share your Canva photos in a variety of ways. If you have or are on a team, you may also share your opinions with them.

Sharing from Within the Editor Using Links

If you provide a link to your design that just allows comments, people may see all of the comments in the editor without signing in. One must register or log in before they may respond, make new notes, or alter the plan.

Computer

- Download and open the design you want to distribute.
- From the menu bar above the notepad, choose Share.
- You can choose who to share with using the drop-down box next to the Collaboration link. You may share the URL with anybody, your team (only Canva Teams users), or all users. The style that is selected by default may only be altered by you.
- You may choose whether to grant the ability to edit, write, or see. After that, you may alter the rights anytime you'd want.
- Select the "Copy" link.

Mobile

- Launch the design that you want to distribute.
- Above the editor, tap the Share icon.
- Select the "Share" link .
- The dropdown menu next to the Collaboration link allows you to choose who you want to share with. You have the option to share the link with everybody, only your team (for Canva Teams users only), or just yourself. You are the only one who can access the default style.
- On the other option, you may choose whether to grant the ability to read, write, or modify. You are free to modify the rights at any time after this.
- Select the "Copy" link.

Why Does My Design Contain Unknown or Guest Users?

If you see "guest users" in your design, certain persons with the design link can make modifications. These folks will have photos and names of animals. This allows users to make changes without having to register or log in.

Sharing from the Home Page Using Links

Computer

- Locate the drawing you want to share from a folder or the Canva home page.
- Drag your mouse pointer over its image and choose the "More" icon that appears. Another option is to just click on the concept.
- Select "Share ."
- The dropdown menu next to the Collaboration link allows you to choose who you want to share with. You may share the URL with anybody, your team (only Canva Teams users), or all users. You are the only one who can access the default style.
- On the other option, you may choose whether to grant the ability to read, write, or modify. You are free to modify the rights at any time after this.
- Select the "Copy" link.

Mobile

- Locate the picture you want to share in Projects or your files.
- Tap the "More" button on the picture you want to share. Another option is to just click on the concept.

- Select "Share."
- The dropdown menu next to the Collaboration link allows you to choose who you want to share with. You may share the URL with anybody, your team (only Canva Teams users), or all users. You are the only one who can access the default style.
- The other selection allows you to choose the kind of privileges you want to grant: can, edit, write, or view. You are free to modify the rights at any time after this.
- Select the "Copy" link.

Using Email to Share With Certain Individuals

You may make your thoughts visible to certain individuals by providing their email addresses.

Computer

- Download and open the design you want to distribute.
- After the editor opens, go to the menu bar. Click Share after that.
- Enter the email addresses of the people you want to share your artwork with in the text area. Commas must be used to separate them. You may search for their name and add them immediately if you're on a team.
- You may choose whether the individual can read, write, or change from the drop-down box. After that, you may alter the rights anytime you'd want.
- Press Send.

Mobile

- Download and open the design you want to distribute.
- At the top of the window, click the Share option.
- Click the "Share" button.
- Enter the email addresses of the people you want to share your artwork with in the text area. Commas must be used to separate them. You may search for their name and add them immediately if you're on a team.
- You may choose whether the individual can read, write, or change from the drop-down box. After that, you may alter the rights anytime you'd want.
- Select "Send." Profile Picture Sharing

Designs that have previously been shared with other users are available for users to choose from. If you click on your own photo, you can see who can see your folder or design.

- You are the only one who can view a design or location without a photo of you.

✦ It will include two group photographs if it is shared with several individuals or teams.

A "+" symbol will appear next to the second personal photo if the design is shared with more than two individuals. This implies that it is available for usage by you and a minimum of two other individuals or groups.

Export artwork that is print-ready

Step One: Produce Your Art

On Canva's home screen, click "Create a Design" in the top right corner. This is the screen you'll see; you may either start your design from scratch or utilize a template.

Step two: Locate the "Download" section

Once your concept is complete, you must share your artwork. In the upper right corner of your screen, click the "Share" icon. Click "Download."

Step three: Modify Your Export Preferences for PDF Exports

- Select "PNG" to see the further options. The most probable option for your File Type is "PNG." The most crucial step is to confirm that the file type you are using is "PDF (Print)."

- The finest prints will be obtained in this situation. Note: The Standard and Print PDFs have differing output quality and "crop mark" and "color mode" settings. Since Stark doesn't employ crop marks, you don't have to make this decision if you're sending us artwork. Instead, we use flow.

Choosing the Color Mode

If you are using a different printer, they may need crop marks. To find out what settings your printer wants you to use, speak with it again. However, choosing a hue is a crucial step in this procedure. Your artwork must be in CMYK color when printed. For computer files such as this one (a blog entry or a social network post), RGB is the color mode.

Important: If you use Canva's free edition, you can only share your artwork in RGB. Our Prepress Team can adjust the color mode for you, so don't worry. Remember that there can be minor color changes in your work. Neons and vivid hues may not seem as bright. Sending artwork as a PDF is the most effective approach to prepare it for printing. The artwork may still be altered in this manner. You could still be able to alter it using other graphic design tools, depending on the visuals (text, photos, or other vector graphics) in your artwork.

The "Flatten PDF" option should not be checked. You may use Canva to turn your artwork into a single image by checking this box. No text or images from the original version of your artwork may be altered. Additionally, you may alter the text if you submit your artwork as a PDF without flattening it. It is important to note that some styles on Canva are not open source, meaning that anybody cannot use them. There can be an additional cost if we need to alter your artwork to fit that style. If you choose not to pay the license costs for the original typeface or fonts, there is no additional cost. We can always locate a font that is similar for you. There is nothing further to do once you have finished setting up! The PDF may be uploaded directly to your payment once you click "Download."

Designs for Printing

+ Launch the PDF file that you have stored on your PC.
+ Click the Print button or printer icon on your PDF reader. You may also use Ctrl + P (Windows) or Command + P (Mac) to print.
+ The kind of printer you own is up to you. Verify if it can resize the image to the desired size.
+ Verify the configuration of your printer. Make sure your photo prints correctly by setting it to 100% scale.
+ To print, click the Print button.

Activities

1. File Types Supported for Download
2. Sharing from the Home Page Using Links
3. Using Email to Share With Certain Individuals

CHAPTER THIRTEEN
SOLVING DESIGN PROBLEMS AND PROVIDING ADVICE

Typical Problems and Their Fixes

Crashing or freezing on Canva

Your internet connection, your browser's lag, or the complexity of your design is likely the causes of Canva stopping or crashing while you're working. Initially, confirm that you are able to connect to the internet. For Canva to load templates, save your work, and function properly, a reliable network is essential. Restart your computer or go to a different network if your internet is sluggish. To gain a better connection if you're using Wi-Fi, you may want to go closer to the router. Next, empty your browser's cache. Over time, cached files may cause browser lag or reduce the functionality of online programs like Canva. Examine the privacy settings of your browser and clear the cache and cookies. Restart Canva when you're finished and continue working. Any unnecessary tabs or background apps should be closed if Canva is still sluggish or unresponsive. They can be depleting the resources of your system. Switching platforms may also resolve compatibility issues. For example, try opening Canva on Chrome or Edge if you're experiencing issues with it in Safari. Don't any of these steps work? To clear off any small issues, restart your computer and start afresh. Simplify your design as a precaution. Large designs with a lot of high-resolution photos or components can be too much for Canva to manage. Reduce the number of elements or compress the images to lighten the file.

Problems with Image Uploads

Sometimes the size, structure, or speed of the connection makes it difficult to upload images to Canva. First, confirm that your image is in a usable file type, such as PNG, JPEG, or SVG. If the image is in an unapproved format, such as RAW, it will not upload. To convert it to a format that works, you'll need to use an image editor or a free program like Convertio. Uploading huge files either takes longer or doesn't function at all. To remedy this, compress your image using programs like TinyPNG. This will reduce the size of the file without sacrificing quality. This not only facilitates sharing but also speeds up Canva as a whole. If your photo still won't upload, check the file name. Special characters like "@," "#," or "&" might sometimes make file sharing challenging. Choose a name for the file that consists of simple characters and numbers. Reopen the Canva editor if the file still doesn't function after completing these procedures. You may simply drag and drop the image directly into the design to prevent any upload issues. Finally, make sure you have a robust internet connection. Downloads may be stopped by an unreliable connection.

Incorrect Display of Fonts

Compatibility issues with font files or computer speed are often the source of font display issues. Make sure that any custom fonts you publish are in one of the TrueType Font (TTF) or OpenType Font (OTF) formats that Canva supports. Try submitting it again in Canva's Brand Kit part if the font file type is correct yet it doesn't appear. Errors occur when the upload procedure doesn't always end properly. Reload the Canva page after clearing your browser's cache and cookies if the fonts are still not looking correct. Cache data may interfere with web applications' ability to load resources, such as fonts. Verify the text box's settings if there are display issues with a design, such as non-straight writing. Adjust the line height, letter spacing, and font size to correct the appearance. To rule out compatibility issues, you might want to try a different browser if these fixes don't resolve the issue.

Problems with Alignment

The design may appear sloppy when elements in Canva, such as text, images, or shapes, don't line up correctly. Turn on gridlines or guides from the "File" menu in the editor to correct this. You can precisely position items with the aid of these visual aids. As you move items around, Canva's snap-to-grid feature will automatically align them with the nearest guide. This maintains everything's position. Group items together when working with multiple items that must remain in the same relationship. To accomplish this, select every element you wish to retain together, then right-click and select "Group." You can move or resize them without losing their positions because this will lock their positions. To make minor adjustments, use the keyboard's arrow keys. They enable precise placement, down to the last pixel. Parts that overlap unintentionally can occasionally cause alignment issues. Using Canva's layer controls, you can alter the arrangement of stacked items. If, for example, a text box is obscured by an image, send the image to the back layer or move the text to the front.

Download Problems

Problems with downloading in Canva might include downloads that don't function or files that are in the incorrect format. First, check sure your internet connection is steady if you can't download a design. For Canva to operate and transfer files, it requires a solid connection. Go back to the page and attempt acquiring it again. If the download still doesn't work, make the design simpler by cutting down on the amount of pieces or high-resolution photos that are utilized. It is extremely crucial to pick the proper file format for downloads to operate. When it comes to photographs, PNG is preferable for high-quality pictures whereas JPG files are smaller. Depending on what you require, choose PDF Standard or PDF Print for your files. If any elements of the saved file are missing, make sure that all fonts, pictures, and other resources are loaded in the editor before you export. If you still have difficulty, try a different browser or device. There are situations when short-term difficulties with your present configuration might make the download process less seamless. Last but not least, you may seek for assistance from Canva's support staff by outlining the issue and submitting your design file.

Background Remover Not Working

Canva Pro members can utilize the Background Remover tool; however it doesn't always function well, particularly with photographs that are sophisticated. Select an image with a lot of contrast so that the subject and background may be easily distinguished if the program fails to remove the backdrop appropriately. This makes it easier for Canva's AI to determine what should be removed. You may use the "Restore" brush to gently restore back any pieces of the topic that the tool removes. If there are remnants of the backdrop, you may use the "Erase" brush to smooth off the edges. Before importing the image into Canva, you may want to use an external application like Remove.bg to get rid of the backdrop if you're using the free plan.

Time-saving advice

- **Start by using templates:** Canva's templates are one feature that really helps me save time. Rather of beginning from scratch, start with a template that meets your design objectives. Canva provides hundreds of expertly created templates for resumes, presentations, posters, social media posts, and more. You may search for templates using relevant keywords or just browse by category, and then modify the text, images, and colors to make it uniquely yours. Making plans this manner saves time and produces a better final product.
- **Establish a Brand Kit:** If you create a lot of graphics for your company or personal brand, Canva's Brand Kit feature may save you a ton of time. You may keep your typefaces in one location and add the colors and graphics of your brand there. Once your name Kit is set up, you can add your name to any design with a few clicks. Using templates, for example, allows you to swiftly alter the

colors and designs to fit the preferences of your business. Your projects will all have the same appearance in this manner.

+ **Make Use of the "Magic Resize" Utility:** For Canva Pro users, the Magic Resize tool is what makes all the difference. It enables you to modify a design to accommodate varying sizes without having to start from scratch. For instance, the Magic Resize tool can adjust the sizes for you if you create a Facebook post and then want to use the same design on Instagram or Twitter. You may need to make a few minor adjustments, but it's a lot quicker than beginning from scratch.

+ **Keep Frequently Used Components Safe:** Using the same components in many projects on Canva might save you time. To make it easier to access frequently used text boxes, icons, or photos, place them in a folder dedicated to them. Additionally, you may create a design template for repetitive tasks, such as emails or social media postings, and then use it again as needed. This eliminates the need for you to recreate the formatting or style every time. **Acquire knowledge of keyboard shortcuts: Gaining proficiency with Canva's computer shortcuts can greatly speed up your work. For instance:**
  ➤ To copy and paste items, use Ctrl+C (or Command+C on a Mac).
  ➤ To undo an activity, use Ctrl+Z; to redo an action, press Ctrl+Shift+Z.
  ➤ For precise modifications, swiftly align items using the Ctrl+Arrow keys.
  ➤ Using more shortcuts in your everyday life can help you work more quickly.

+ **Duplicate Pages or Designs:** You don't have to start from scratch on every page when creating a series of designs that have a common structure, such as show slides. Canva allows you to replicate certain pages or whole designs with a single click. This is highly beneficial for maintaining consistency and saving time on repetitive tasks.

+ **Make Effective Use of Canva's Search Function:** You may access components, layouts, and photos without having to browse Canva's extensive collection. Use precise phrases in the search box instead. Adding filters such as theme, color, or style may improve the results. For instance, search for "minimalist" with the icon type (e.g., "minimalist phone icon") if you want a minimalist icon.

+ **Arrange Your Tasks:** You can maintain the organization of your designs in Canva by using folders. Jobs may be categorized by kind, including presentations, social media, and client work. Keeping everything organized will help you find specific designs or files more quickly.

+ **Make Use of Pre-Set Measurements:** For the majority of projects, such as A4 documents, LinkedIn banners, and Instagram posts, Canva has predetermined sizes. By selecting the appropriate sizes up front, you may avoid having to alter your ideas later and save time. You may also create your own dimensions for certain purposes and save them for later use.

- **Work Together Instantaneously:** Your team may collaborate on a project simultaneously by using Canva's real-time collaboration feature. Your colleagues may edit or comment directly on your design after you share it with them. This expedites the review process by eliminating the need to exchange files or send and receive letters.
- **Look for and swap out:** When working on designs with repetitive text, Canva's search-and-replace feature may help you save time. If you need to alter the date or business name in several places in your design, you may use this tool to make changes fast without having to manually update each text box.
- **Use Canva's Content Planner:** If you are in control of social media, you may plan posts directly from the app using Canva's Content Planner. As a result, you won't need to often move between Canva and other scheduling apps. Your material may be simultaneously scheduled and designed.
- **Automate Repetitive Tasks with Canva Pro:** When you upgrade to Canva Pro, you can utilize features like the Background Remover and Magic Resize that may make projects that would typically take time quicker. For example, manually removing the backdrop may take a lot of effort, while Canva's tool just requires one click. Similarly, it is simple to adjust the size of designs for various devices using Pro tools.
- **Maintain a Clean Workspace:** Cleaning up your Canva workstation will ultimately save you time. Store outdated designs in folders or put them aside to make your dashboard easier to use. You can locate what you need and begin new tasks more quickly if you keep your workspace tidy.

Conclusion

Canva is a robust and intuitive design tool that makes it easy for both novices and experts to produce eye-catching images. Users may create professional-quality designs for a variety of uses, including presentations, marketing materials, business cards, and social media graphics, by experimenting with its wide range of tools, templates, and capabilities. Canva's value is in its capacity to streamline the design process, making it usable by those without any previous design knowledge while providing sophisticated functionality for more experienced producers. A productive and easy workflow is guaranteed by its user-friendly drag-and-drop interface, editable templates, and seamless platform connection. Utilize Canva's features, such brand kits, animation choices, and collaboration tools, to improve your designs as you continue to explore it.

Try different layouts, typefaces, and components to find your own creative voice. Keep in mind that practice and studying Canva's many resources are the keys to mastering it. Canva provides the versatility and resources you need to realize your ideas, whether you're creating for commercial, personal, or professional use. Accept the creative freedom it offers and allow your creations to leave a lasting impression.

INDEX